Pastels

from scratch

Pastels

from scratch

Art Workshop with Paul

Paul Taggart

Sandcastle
Books

First Published in Great Britain in 2006 by
Sandcastle Books Limited
The Stables
Sheriffs Lench Court
Sheriffs Lench
Nr. Evesham
Worcs. WR11 4SN

www.sandcastlebooks.co.uk

ISBN 0-9552478-3-7

Printed and bound in Thailand

Contents

Pastel
PRINCIPLES

Pastel is a pure and radiant medium, whose beauty is reliant on its intense pigmentation. When fully harnessed, the unique characteristics of pastels will furnish any artist with an array of techniques that far outstrip the common view of this medium. Not surprising that pastel painting takes so many by surprise when they discover its full potential.

The principles of pastel painting can take you on a journey from the simplest of chalky sketches through to a masterpiece that has been painstakingly built up in layers of graduated colours, working from intense darks to dazzling lights.

To work with pastels is to work with a medium that is unique, in that it can be exploited not only in its dry state, but also be manipulated in wet form. Moreover, the range of techniques and possibilities can be extended even further, through bringing other media, such as watercolours, into play.

Contrary to popular belief, sticks of pastels are not unwieldy and are perfectly capable of yielding the finest of strokes and tiniest of accents. As such, this medium is equally capable of rendering dainty subjects, as it is bold, dramatic paintings.

Blended and gently graduating colours are fully exploited to suggest the light and volume of a magnificent yellow rose bloom – pages 62 to 67

The principles of Pastels from Scratch will introduce you to this captivating medium, focussing on two types of pastel – sketching pastels and Artists' Quality soft pastels. You will experience the versatility of each and begin your journey of discovery into an array of possibilities.

The process of learning to paint in any medium cannot be hurried and as with any new pursuit, it is important to set time aside to absorb all this new information. Be forgiving with yourself throughout the process of learning how to handle pastels and your sense of self-fulfilment will come naturally.

Basic instruction, coupled with simple exercises, form the initial tutorials on pastel types, pastel blenders, palettes of pastel colours and a variety of surfaces suitable for use in pastel painting. Follow these various exercises and Artstrips covering different tools and techniques.

The rich lustrous pigments in Artists' Quality soft pastels bring a vividly coloured Mediterranean building to life – pages 36 and 37

It is important to understand that when working on the exercises, they need not be perfect. Be patient with yourself, no-one has ever learned to paint without making mistakes, time and again.

Artists' pastels are a far throw from the chalks with which most of us are familiar, or the phrase 'pastel colours'. Unlike the washed-out pastel colours of everyday parlance, artists' pastel colours are a treasure trove of brilliant jewel colours. In pastel painting an artist is working with the most intense pigments available in any medium.

The reflective qualities of transparent objects prove invaluable in learning how the values of a colour are as important as its hue – pages 50 to 55

Partners to the basics are a series of projects. Intended to extend your development, these take you on to the next stage through an initial exercise, followed by a stage-by-stage painting. The finished studies and paintings are not only meant to be inspirational and challenging, they also demonstrate the versatility of pastels.

However, as with the basics, do not be concerned should your results not resemble those in the book. Remember, it is not the outcome that matters in the early days of painting; it is how you follow the process and what you experience as a consequence.

All too often lack of confidence restricts a person's ability to develop, largely brought about by setting high goals of achievement from the outset. This rapidly leads to frustration and self-doubt. Rather than have such expectations, it is far better to enjoy the process of discovery and give yourself a fighting chance.

As an introduction to pastel painting for beginners and painters alike, the purpose of Pastels from Scratch is to demystify this unique medium and to demonstrate how stimulating pastels can be.

The beauty of pastel painting lies not only in its intense hues, but also in its painterly characteristics and falls neatly between the art of drawing and that of painting.

Artists' soft pastels offer the painter a full range of colours and are almost entirely composed of pure pigment, a fine powder bound together with the barest amount of glue, then formed into sticks. When applied to the surface, the view of this unsullied pigment, unlike its wet paint counterparts, is not marred by an encapsulating film of medium. As a consequence a pastel painted surface seems almost to glow with the intensity of the applied pigment.

Although a dry medium, working with pastels nevertheless has the characteristic of painting, through the ability to build up layers of colour as in painting with oils, or acrylics.

As layers of soft pastels are overlaid, the surface begins to feel fluid, when the particles of pigment slip, slide and mix together. Colours on the surface can be blended together in much the same manner as paint; pastel strokes can be applied in much the same manner as brush-stroke.

The result is a juicy, painterly work of art, vibrating with intense colour.

Since the dawn of humanity, people have been motivated to make marks on surfaces. They must have been driven to do this, for it is no easy matter to collect the raw materials with which to create the pigments required to make such marks. Over the centuries artists have passionately sought out the purest pigments, the brightest colours. Painters of today are blessed with access to colours that range across the entire spectrum, made from the purest and most intense pigments garnered from around the world and there is no more startling a range of hues than those available to the pastel painter.

A full colour palette, including pastels of varying colour temperatures, is maximised to render the far-reaching depths within a receding landscape – pages 74 to 79

Which pastels do I need?

The first time you lay your hands on an Artists' Quality soft pastel it will become obvious that you are looking at something really special. Open a drawer filled with these pastels and it is like lifting the lid on a chest of jewels, for the colours are dazzling in their intensity.

Sticks of Artists' Quality soft pastels are pure pigment held together with just enough gum to hold them in shape. They stand apart from watercolours, oils and acrylics, which consist of pigment mixed with a medium (gum) that is required to hold them to the surface.

WHAT IS A DRY PASTEL AND WHY SHOULD IT BE SOFT?

The gum in pastels is, merely added to form the powdered pigment into 'tools' with which the dry pigment can be applied to the surface. As the sticks are drawn across the surface, the gum shatters and the pastel literally disintegrates, laying the pigment powder onto the surface. Applying pressure to the sticks forces the pastel powder into the texture (tooth) of the surface. The pigment powder now relies on the tooth to hold it to the surface.

There are certain instances where a form of glue is applied, once the pastel has been laid, to protect that layer. This is referred to as fixing, where the pastel is literally turned into a wet paint, which, once dried, is fixed to the surface.

However, while the pastel on the surface remains 'dry', we are looking at the purest form of colour available. The aim of most pastel painters is, therefore, to produce a work with the minimum amount of fixing, so that the colours remain at their most intense.

On starting off a collection of Artists' Quality soft pastels, it becomes evident that the degree of softness varies across different makes and ranges. Some are very soft, others less so and a subtle balance has to be achieved.

The more gum added to the sticks, the harder the pastels become and hence they are also stronger. It stands to reason therefore that these more stable pastel sticks are easier to store, handle and transport. The softer the sticks, the more likely they are to crumble, even as they are being applied to the surface of the painting.

However, the softest of pastels require less pressure to apply them to the surface and spread them. The more reduced the amount of pressure needed, the less likely that previously laid layers of pastel will be disturbed by subsequently applied layers – thus affording the pastel painter the opportunity to build up more layers.

The ideal degree of softness is a personal choice and as with the preferred selection of any materials, is developed through usage and experience.

Whilst Artists' Quality soft pastels are those which should be aimed for, there are other options for starting out in this medium. The harder, soft pastel contains less pure pigment and features progressively more chalky fillers. When laid side by side, the difference in colour intensity across the various ranges and types becomes evident. The cheaper pastels tend to look more pastel-like, the colours tend to be softer and less intense. Furthermore, a greater quantity of gum is used to bind the cheaper pastel sticks, which renders them harder and stronger.

This does not mean however that the cheaper pastels should be avoided. Even the most basic, thin chalks can be made to look intense, when they have something against which to shine. For pastel colours are usually worked over a coloured surface.

Which leads us on to another important characteristic of pastels; they are opaque, which means that one colour can completely overpaint another.

In pastels the artist has a medium that is totally forgiving. Not only are mistakes easily rectified, but colours can be layered. It is easy to build these layers from dark

towards light. This is one of the most natural ways to work, as the lower dark colours that represent shadows can be softened.

As the layers are lightened the focus can be progressively sharpened, until the final highlights are applied – the most focussed points of light. Thus, one of the most difficult aspects of painting is overcome immediately, what to do with the shadows. Shadows become the areas that are left behind, as the layers move on towards the lighter values.

The main stumbling block for those starting off in pastels is usually the fact that there is too much choice. Which type of pastels to start with? What colours will be required?

The best advice is to start off small. Overburden yourself with a multitude of colours and you will probably never use them all. A stick of pastel can have a surprisingly long life and will prove expensive if never used.

The following pages deal with two basic types of dry pastel. The first, which I term the soft sketching pastel, is relatively inexpensive and you should familiarise yourself with their properties described in the Artstrips, to ensure you acquire the correct type.

These are used on their own and in conjunction with Artists' Quality soft pastels, in order that you can experience the differences between them and their respective strengths.

Understanding pastels

Basic types

SKETCHING PASTELS
Semi-hard. Sets comprise of limited palette with black and white. Colours are also available individually.

ARTSTRIPS ©

Can be sharpened to a fine point with a pencil sharpener or sharp knife.

Flat end or point of pastel stick is used to produce line-work. Line varies in quality and width as pastel blunts during use.

Strokes of varying width are achieved by working with broader surface of the pastel.

Pastels are very responsive, enabling descriptive and diverse qualities of marks to be achieved by varying direction and pressure of strokes.

Similar dry 'sketching' pastels are available in round sticks. Will work in same manner as square versions.

The majority of would-be pastel painters begin with a starter set of sketching pastels. Rather than make the most common mistake of attempting to use every colour in a set for each piece of work, it is better to begin with one or two colours. This will help you to discover and explore the character of pastel. For example, how good a line can you achieve and how soon does a sharpened point wear down? What qualities does a stroke of pastel possess and how does this change when applied to different surfaces?

An exercise comprising one principal colour, with accents produced using a second, can be very effective. It will teach you to exploit the colour values (lights and darks) to their utmost, using one colour alone. Moving on to a second, darker, colour to accent certain areas then becomes a bonus, which will prove far more exciting. There is nothing that will reward you more than patience, when it comes to the build up of pastel layers.

Basic types

ARTISTS' QUALITY SOFT ROUND – made from pure colour (dry pigment) to which a little gum solution is added - then rolled into sticks.

ARTSTRIPS ©

Each colour is available in a range of values. These are tints that denote the progressive addition of white pigment.

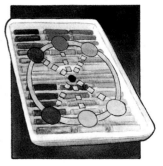

Since colour mixing with a 'dry' medium is less efficient than with wet paint, it is helpful to work with a range of both primary and secondary colours.

Artists' Quality soft dry pastels are so soft, that when gently run across the palm they will leave a mark. This is their secret…

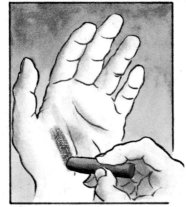

…being so soft, virtually no pressure is required to overpaint in layers. Essential to produce rich pastel paintings.

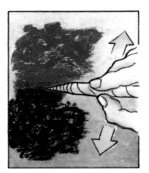

Ideal for softly blending on the surface, using finger or blender.

A full range of values is required to achieve volume, light and depth, so each colour is produced in a range of tints.

Better to start with a few colours in a full range of tints, plus black and white.

When extending the set of pastels, a full range of tints should be included for each colour added.

Pastels in practice

SKETCHING PASTELS
SQUARE OR ROUND

The sharpened point or edge at the tip of a square, or round, soft sketching pastel stick produces soft coloured line-work. These colours can be mixed together on the surface by hatching different hues next to each other. Hatching coloured strokes has the advantage of allowing the colour of the surface to show through to play a large part in the finished sketch. These more basic pastels are less suitable for working over one another, being harder than the Artists' Quality pastels. Nevertheless, some limited overlaying is possible.

Presenting the side of the pastel stick to the surface produces a broad stroke. In this sketch the strokes have been left raw in an unblended state, in order that their character can be easily seen. Changing the direction of strokes can vary the width of them considerably, until they become very fluid and irregular [brown strokes at the bottom]. Vary the pressure for differing strengths of colour [bridge]. Only a few layers of overlay are possible.

ARTISTS' QUALITY SOFT PASTELS

These pastel sticks provide rich deposits of pigment. For this sketch the end of a pastel stick is used to complete the outline. Once the outline is completed use a compressed paper stump to smear the pigment from the outline across the rest of the surface. It will become immediately apparent how important the direction of the blend becomes as it 'carves' out the headland into definite planes. So much pigment is picked up by the stump that this alone can be used to deposit enough pigment in the sky to begin the clouds.

NOTE

GREAT CARE MUST BE TAKEN NOT TO EXERT TOO MUCH PRESSURE WHEN USING THESE SOFT PASTELS STICKS, AS THE SURFACE CAN SOON BE OVERWHELMED.

In this sketch the Artists' Quality soft pastels are used to build up layers of colour, stroke over stroke. A heavily textured paper was selected to demonstrate the influence of a surface on the strokes. In this instance blending is not employed for two reasons. Firstly to prevent the surface texture from being obliterated and secondly, to explore how many layers of pastel can be overlaid without resorting to blending and fixing.

Exercise for pastels

▶ **Use sketching pastels to complete** outline drawing in light brown and fill gently with local, dark dull colours. Blend vigorously with a compressed paper stump, until they resemble soft washes of colour. Having been pushed into the paper tooth these are very stable. This sketching pastel layer is completed with a black pastel line drawing, again pushed home with the stump.

◀ **Switch to Artists' Quality soft pastels** to provide more powerful coverage and stronger darks. Colours should be kept as cool as possible to provide a contrast for the sunlight to come. These early dark layers should be blended gently to keep focus soft within the shadows.

▶ **Now work with warm colours** – those with plenty of yellow and orange in them – to suggest the rays of sunlight as they penetrate the cool shadows. There is no blending at this stage; instead, depend on a variety of different pressures and directions in each pastel stroke.

For this exercise both sketching and Artists' Quality *pastels* have been brought together. Being harder, the sketching pastels can easily be sharpened to a point and are thus extremely useful for the early stages of drawing. However, since it is not possible to build as many layers with these, later use of the Artists' Quality soft pastels extends the range of values and hues available to complete this study.

Taking into account the different pressures required to apply each type of pastel, it makes sense to begin with the harder sketching pastels and finish off with the Artists' Quality. Working in this manner means that you are exploiting the best qualities of both types of pastel, while taking into account their respective limitations. The result is a perfect blend of temperament, which allows both controlled drawing and vivid colour.

Why do I need different blenders?

Pastel painting is unlike any of the wet media, in that the pastel stick itself is used to deliver the pigment to the painting surface. Once applied, however, it can be manipulated very much in the same manner as paint on canvas or watercolour paper.

This is why I refer to working with pastels as 'pastel painting'. At first this may seem a strange description for a medium that is generally kept completely dry. Nevertheless, it is the process of moving the pastel about on the surface, in a very fluid manner, which evokes the painting process, particularly that of oil painting.

THE NATURAL QUALITY OF A PASTEL STROKES is dictated by two elements. First, the softness of the pastel stick determines the quantity of pigment deposited and the pressure needed to produce that particular stroke. Second, the tooth, or texture of the surface provides a pattern that the stroke discovers.

Some surfaces have a linear quality, while others may feature a woven, honeycomb, or granular pattern and so on. The dominance of any surface is revealed within the first few strokes and although these characteristics can be exciting, they do have to be curtailed and controlled to allow the pastel marks to achieve their full potential.

Pastel strokes are hard-edged and broken by the surface texture. Further down the line, these perforated strokes will enable us to see down through the layers of colour, but initially, especially on uniformly patterned surfaces, they can be distracting.

The first instinct is to use one's finger to smear these strokes into and across the surface. This form of blending is quite acceptable, although a little messy!

A cleaner and more controlled method of blending is to use a brush. A stiff brush will be aggressive, forcing pigment into and across the tooth of the surface. However, it will also simultaneously dislodge more pastel than a softer, more flexible brush. It is therefore important to select the right brush to achieve the required effect.

Blenders specifically designed for use in pastel painting include the more traditional rolled paper wipers and compressed paper stumps, both of which come into use within exercises and projects in this book.

Modern innovations, such as rubber-tipped rigid blenders, featuring a variety of differently shaped heads and degree of flexibility can also be added to the range of blenders at an artist's disposal.

These blenders are the 'brushes' of pastel painting, they work the colour across the surface after it has been deposited. The question is – why exactly would you need to do this?

Being hard-edged, pastel strokes tend to appear static and two-dimensional. By blurring these strokes through blending, depth and movement is suggested.

Blending the interior of the pastel stroke fills in any irregularities caused by the surface beneath and renders the stroke more solid, or complete. Continued blending will spread the pigment more thinly across the surface, making it more transparent.

Heavier blending has different effects, dependent on the surface beneath. Should the ground be paper, the pastel will become more firmly embedded in its tooth. This solidifies and strengthens the layer, so that it can more easily accept further pastel layers.

If pastel colour lies below a blended layer, then it will tend to mix, creating a colour mix that will be entirely dependent on the pressure employed to merge the two.

Hard edges of one colour can be merged into that of a neighbour to create a gradation of colour, or different values of a particular colour.

The permutations are enormous and provide pastel painters with a wide repertoire of differing marks, colour possibilities and potential qualities.

Blending is therefore of the utmost importance, as it will allow you to mix colours on the surface and create softness to suggest depth, movement and atmosphere.

Where do you start?
As always it is better to start simply. Although pastels can easily emulate the solid opacity of an oil paint, they can also be employed more thinly, which is the starting point for the exercises in this section.

These studies will suit anyone starting to work with either colour or pastel, since the Line and Wash technique on which they are based is a simple drawing to which a few colours are overlaid.

There are other benefits to this simple approach. First, very few colours are required, which will help you concentrate on the technique, rather than which colour to use. Furthermore, because the underlying drawing describes the detail of the flower, colour accuracy and sharpness is not an issue.

Thinly applied pastel is easier to remove, not only to correct mistakes, but more importantly, to be exploited as part of the painting process.

Brush blending

Dry brush blending

On tinted pastel paper, gently sketch in outline with pencil. Use Rigger brush to add some Indian ink descriptive line-work – vary quality and thickness.

ARTSTRIPS ©

With large round oil painter's bristle brush, rub over surface of pastel stick to pick up loose pigment.

Transfer pigment to drawing and work into the surface.

Small brush would give more detailed coverage, but colour runs out quickly. Larger brushes cover greater area and hold more colour.

Use kneadable putty rubber to lift off highlights. This will expose tinted paper beneath – so highlights will be coloured.

Add final white highlights with pastel stick. This will contrast with the tinted paper.

The result, using this method, is reminiscent of the Line and Wash technique in watercolour painting, except that it is 'dry'. A simple process that requires the minimum of equipment – ideal for pastel sketching out of doors.

The pastel provides gentle layers of pigment across the base colour of the tinted pastel paper. So extended is the colour, that in spite of the pastel's natural opacity, it does not obliterate the ink line. In fact, the colour over the ink serves to enhance the quality of the black detailing.

The tinted paper colour is exploited to the full, both through the thin layers of pastel, where it is exposed, once erased and as a backdrop to the composition as whole.

Wet brush blending

Sketch and ink in outline as before. Use pastel stick to apply colour directly to the surface, Will result in much heavier application of colour.

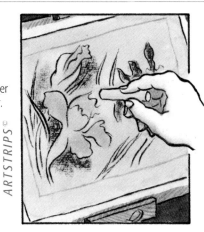

ARTSTRIPS ©

With large round soft brush, apply water to the surface to spread pastels up to the edges of the outline.

Applying water thins out the pastel and allows line-work to show through.

Leave to dry before adding a lighter colour using same technique.

Should the idea of a painterly technique appeal (working fluid colour over the surface with a brush) this method is, yet again, a simple one, that requires little by way of equipment.

The pigment found in pastel is the same as that in paint, but without the more generous amounts of gum that act like a glue. Although some pastel painters in the past have been known to dissolve pastel pigment using the steam from a boiling kettle, this process relies on a far less dangerous method!

A wet, soft round brush is employed to dissolve and spread the colour. This spreads the pigment more evenly into the tooth of the pastel paper, than would be physically possible with the dry pastel. Once again, the ink line-work, can show through effectively.

The very low level of gum in the mix means that once the water evaporates away, the pastel remains quite powdery on the surface. It is therefore possible to erase and blend further, wherever necessary.

Blending and soft brushwork in the laying of the colour brings the finished quality even closer to that of Line and Wash and is a very pleasant introduction to the use of gentle pastel colour.

> **TIPS:**
> Always clean brushes at the end of a painting session.
> When drying a brush out, stand it in a jar, never on its head.
> Brushes made of natural hair must be protected against moth attack.

Exercise for dry brush blending

Preparation

Most pastel papers tend to be a little thin in comparison to watercolour paper. Applied pastel strokes are therefore inclined to pick up irregularities in the underlay beneath the pastel paper. While this is sometimes exploited, more often than not it proves to be frustrating. The solution is to place an underlay of newspaper, or smooth card, between the pastel paper and the drawing board.

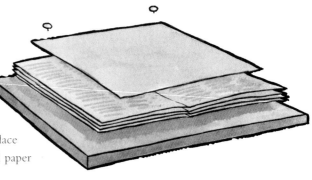

> **TIP**
> When working over previously applied pastel, with either pastel or brush, it is easy to smudge the surface. This becomes more apparent as the layers of colour are built up. Fixing the pastel is not an option when further blending or erasing is required, as neither would be possible with fixed pastel. The solution is a simple mask of clean smooth paper, placed beneath your hand. Pastel can take downward pressure, without much damage occurring. It is sideways friction that causes applied pastel to be dislodged and smeared.

Line-work

The quality of line-work is an essential element in this technique. A wide choice of different tools are available that will provide a vast range of line characteristics. It is important to ensure that the ink being used is lightfast. Options include (from the top down):-

Rigger brush
Brush pen
Dip pen
Drawing pen
Fibre tip pen
Felt tip pen
Small round brush
Medium round brush
Large round brush

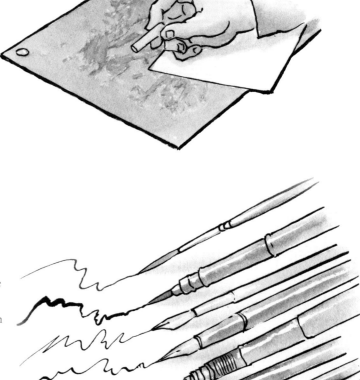

This exercise will suit those who are still a little nervous of venturing into painting itself, but want to begin experimenting with colour. I consider this to be one of the first stepping-stones into both pastel and paint.

In this study the pastel is applied dry, using a bristle brush. While the effect of soft colour and hard line-work visually resembles the watercolour technique of Line and Wash, the physical application of pigment is much stiffer.

The ground on which the work is produced is not the stark white of watercolour paper. The colour of the tinted pastel paper will modify the overlaid pastel colours and is therefore exploited to provide a contrast to strong colours, whilst simultaneously harmonizing the thin layers of colour.

NOTE – HOW THE COMPLEMENTARY COLOURS OF RED AND GREEN ARE HELD TOGETHER BY THE WARM COLOUR BENEATH. IN CONTRAST, THE WHITE HIGHLIGHTS CREATE A PERFECT FOIL FOR THE INTENSLEY DARK ACCENTS OF THE LINE-WORK - SHINING OUT AGAINST THE PINK.

Exercise for wet brush blending

◀ **SYMMETRY** The frills of the flower petals can obscure the simplicity of their underlying structure. However, careful observation will reveal their symmetry.

Hold a pencil in front of the subject and rotate until the shaft of the pencil appears to cut the head in half. This is the line of symmetry [red].

Easily seen on the curled yellow bud and just as clearly defined on the more complex blue flower head.

◀ **NEGATIVE SPACE** The shape of the space around the subject [solid dark area] is as important as the shape of the subject itself [solid white area].

By being constantly aware of these forms, you will be able to balance any composition within the containing outer rectangle.

Most importantly, this insight will also enable you to better judge the relationship between the various elements within any composition.

As a general rule – a subject with an interesting negative space will engage the eye more successfully.

◀ **COUNTERCHANGE** Becoming aware of the importance of negative shapes leads on to the use of counterchange. Since using pigment provides a smaller tonal range than is found in light itself, we must constantly look for methods of creating extra contrasts at the edges of objects.

NOTE – THE LIGHT FLOWER HEAD WORKS WELL AGAINST A DARK BACKGROUND. THE DARK BLUE FLOWER HOWEVER, NEEDS A LIGHT BACKGROUND – THE NEGATIVE SPACES AROUND ITS PETALS ARE THEREFORE LIGHTENED (NEGATIVELY RENDERED).

Yellow flowers are notoriously difficult to paint, since whatever colour is added to make them darker, tends to also dull them. As the colours within a flower head remain intense, even into the shadows, this can be frustrating.

In this exercise there are two immediate advantages to working with pastels.

First, the colour of the paper, which can be used as an undercolour. In this instance, a colour from the same family as the yellow has been selected. However, there is no reason that a darker or a complementary colour could not be used. Try the exercise on a dark purple paper and see what effect that has on the yellow. Instead of the yellow pigment mixing with the purple, it will stand proud of it, to provide a complementary contrast – the strongest contrast of colour available to an artist.

Second, the pastel itself is opaque and when a burst of colour highlight is required, it can be solidly applied. This will stand out prominently in its intensity and provides that strong 'splash' of colour required to express the powerful colour of the flower head.

Why do I need a palette of colours and a range of tints?

To fully express the nature of light, volume and depth in a painting, every artist requires a means of achieving a whole range of values.

Although pastels can be mixed on the surface of a painting, the capacity to do so is much more limited than when mixing with fluid paint. The pastel painter, working with this dry medium, has therefore to rely on another method; the ability to exploit and manipulate a range of tints that are produced to effect the different values of any particular hue.

GENERALLY, potential pastel painters' first experience with this medium is through the boxed set of pastel sticks. These provide an adequate starting point with which to experiment and get a feel for the unique characteristics of the dry medium.

However it is difficult for the manufacturers to arrive at a range of colours that will suit every taste, or fulfil every expectation. To overcome this hurdle, the contents of some sets are biased towards a specific subject area and marketed as a landscape set, a portrait set, a flower set, etc.

Whilst this goes some way to resolving the dilemma, their limitations will soon lead you to consider building up a palette of pastel hues and tints that meet your own particular needs.

A boxed set is likely to contain the primary colours, red, blue and yellow, plus black and white. It may well contain two reds, two blues and two yellows, which serve to demonstrate that each hue can be warm or cool. However, by their very nature, boxed sets cannot feature the full range of values for each hue.

The wide-ranging possibilities in colour mixing can only be achieved through acquiring individual pastel sticks, from a larger range of colours.

INDIVIDUAL PASTEL STICKS
The extent of the range of available colours varies across the manufacturers and within different qualities of pastels. The finer Artists' Quality soft pastels are likely to offer a more extensive choice. What these feature is a full range of values in any given hue, from the darkest to the lightest.

To this end, the darkest pastels are almost pure pigment. In some ranges a little black is added to give an even deeper value. The hue is then graduated through a range of tints, achieved by progressively adding white to the base pigment.

This may well result in a set of up to six or more pastel sticks in any one particular colour, which are needed by the artist to effect the graduated change from dark to light in that hue.

NUCLEUS PALETTE OF COLOURS

Establishing your palette of colours need not be confusing, nor potentially wasteful through acquiring pastels that you subsequently never use.

It is far better to start with a handful of colours, featuring their range of tints and gradually add to the collection as your repertoire and confidence grows. It will soon become obvious which colours you tend to favour as the nucleus of your colour palette.

Rather than jump into a full spectrum of colours from the outset, you could consider a selection of coloured greys. Through working on a series of exercises using nothing more than coloured greys you will learn much about the importance of light and shade in developing a composition. Added to which these coloured greys will prove invaluable as you develop, when they can be exploited in mixtures, as underpainting layers and even in some over-painting.

HUE, VALUE, TONE
• Hue is a bright primary or secondary colour on the basic colour circle.
• Value is the degree of lightness or darkness of a colour.
• Tone is the degree of lightness or darkness of a neutral grey.

HIGHLIGHTS
The tiny point of light on the surface at which the light source is reflected. This reflected light may be white, or a colour.

ACCENTS
The darkest points of shadow of an object.

Alternatively, you could to move straight into colour, but restricting yourself to a limited palette of hues. The exercise in this section, using nothing more than brown, blue, white and black, will prove invaluable on several levels.

First, by selecting this range of warm browns and cool blues you can colour mix to create greys. Your need for colour will be satisfied, without falling into the common trap of colour overload, where too many are used, which overburden the composition.

Using a limited, tonal palette, such as this, will concentrate your attention on light and shade and how to render it to achieve volume and depth within the composition.

Limiting the colours from which to execute the study means that you will need to exploit the range of tints to their fullest. It is only by so doing that you wil fully comprehend how the gradual build-up of colour is paramount in establishing the different values of a required hue.

You will also become aware of the important role of the coloured ground on which the exercise is produced. The choice of colour can have a profound effect on the finished result, either harmonizing the composition, or used as a contrasting counterfoil. Choose a warm ground and your cool colours will sing out by contrast and vice versa.

As with the coloured greys, the blues and browns selected for this exercise will prove their worth as part of the nucleus of your full-blown colour palette.

The brightly coloured façade of a Mediterranean house provides an excellent subject for the next stage in developing your colour palette. This vignette allows you to focus on the aspect that interests you most, whilst the rest of the study fades out into the background colour of the paper.

The focal area is given more layers of colour, therefore greater depth and detailing. On the other hand, the areas that fade out require less pastel work to give a suggestion of what is there.

Colour palettes in practice

Limited, tonal palette exercise

PALETTE
To comprise of one warm colour [brown] and one cool colour [blue] in several tints, plus black and white.

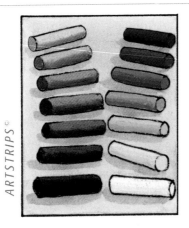

ARTSTRIPS©

DRAWING - Break off small piece of black pastel stick and use to complete initial drawing.

FIRST STAGE - Block in dark masses using both dark blue and dark brown pastels. Work with side or flat end of a piece of each pastel stick.

To stabilise and solidify these masses, use compressed paper stump, to blend colours and force them into the paper texture.

Alternatively, use a cloth or a finger. NOTE – this is less precise.

Re-apply any parts of the drawing that may have disappeared. NOTE – now blend along the line-work, as opposed to across it, to prevent it disappearing once more.

It really is surprising that this limited tonal palette can be sufficient to render any subject, ranging from still-life to landscape, portrait to animal study. The secret lies in two of its assets.

Firstly, you have a range of tints for each colour to work with. Whilst most pastel sets have a range of different hues [colours], they do not, however, possess a range of values [lights and darks]. Without the tonal, or value range, it is very difficult to achieve a sense of depth and light. It is far better to have fewer colours and a larger tonal range, as used in this exercise.

Secondly, this limited, tonal palette is made up of warm and cool colours. All colours possess a colour temperature. For example, red is hot and blue is cool. Although it does not comprise of a wide variety of colours, this palette does feature colour temperatures that can be used in mixes or as contrasts to one another.

The surface can be fixed at this stage to make the next layer easier to apply.

SECOND STAGE – Work right through the picture, successively blocking in lighter blues and browns.

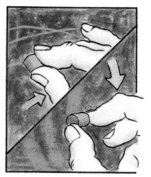

Use sharp edge of pastel stick for line and detail and side for broad marks. Similar to using small and large brushes in painting.

Successively blend more gently as you build up layers of pastel. Use softer rolled paper wipers. Take care, as too much pressure will mix top layers with underlying colours.

FINAL STAGE – Rework with final layers of lightest blues and browns.

Work from top of picture down [from background to foreground]. By overlapping shapes you immediately achieve a sense of depth in the composition.

Note how the warm and cool layers of pastel begin to interact with one another and the colour of the tinted paper beneath. From a few simple layers, the variety of colour mix is enormous. The trick is not to be overenthusiastic in the application of the layers. If you are too heavy handed with the strokes they are likely to obliterate the underlying layers. Although this can prove useful when correcting mistakes, here it will mean that the colour mixes created in the layering process will not show through as they should.

The general rule is to be gentle and restrained. Furthermore, the texture of the paper naturally interrupts the solidity of the pastel strokes, so use this to your advantage as well. Exploit what the pastel does naturally and you will then be working in harmony with the medium.

> **TIP**:
> In limited colour or limited layer renderings, the use of both black and white is essential. Both of these colours can have a dulling effect if applied over generously.
> However, black as an undercolour and white as final spots of highlight will provide the sparkle to these wonderful pastel hues.

TIP - Variations of downward pressure during strokes increases or decreases amount of pigment deposited.

ARTSTRIPS ©

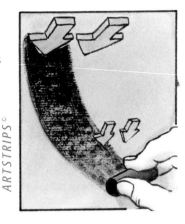

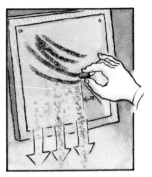

TIP - Blue can be laid over and/or blended and mixed with browns to produce greys.

TIP - Working upright helps to prevent accidental smearing with you hand. Excess loose pastel pigment powder and crumbs simply fall away

FINISHING TOUCHES Apply pure white highlights and black accents to selected areas. These complete the tonal range and are seldom blended.

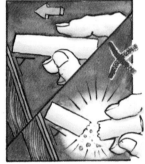

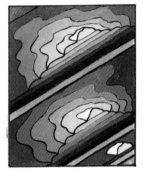

Extra pressure is needed to apply such highlights and accents. Use a complete pastel stick held at a steep angle to avoid breakage.

White highlights over a layered colour appear to be the lightest value of that colour. Against a dark colour they are starkly white.

As the layers of colour overlap and intermix, it can be seen that apart from a temperature range and a tonal range, we are also furnished with a range of differing intensities. In other words, the chosen colours are such opposites [complementaries] to one another, that, when mixed, they have the effect of dulling each other down, to, in effect, produce coloured greys.

Added to this, we have white which, in mixtures, always tends to dull while it lightens. Used in its pure form however, it is the ultimate light contrast [highlight].

Black too, will dull mixtures, but can be used under colours to enrich them. Used in its pure form it provides the ultimate dark contrast [accent].

COLOUR COMPLEMENTARIES and COLOURED GREYS

Brown is a dull orange [an orange already mixed with a little blue]. Its complementary [opposite] on the colour circle is blue.

The coloured greys that are created can have a bias to either the brown or the blue. Effectively, the greys can be warm or cool.

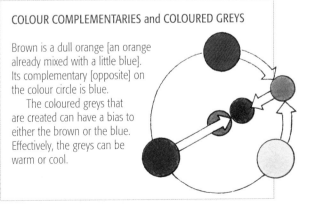

The colour of the tinted paper was carefully chosen for this exercise. Since the finished study is mainly composed of the cool blues of the snow, the warm dull pink of the surface provides an excellent contrast.

Although only tiny specks of this colour are visible in the finished piece, it nevertheless plays an important role in harmonizing the entire composition. The pink surface, in effect, works as a third colour, which can be very important when using a limited palette.

The maximum contrast of black accents against white highlights is restricted to the area around the figures and even though these figures are not described in detail, gives a focal point to the composition.

NOTE – EVEN THOUGH THERE IS LITTLE COLOUR IN THIS EXERCISE, YOUR BRAIN WILL ACTUALLY 'IMAGINE' THERE TO BE MORE COLOUR IN IT, PROVIDING IT FEATURES A FULL TONAL RANGE.

Do not assume therefore that this subject is only suited to the limited palette used here simply because the colours are biased towards the winter scene.

Try this exercise out on a spring, summer or autumn scene and you will be amazed how effective the results are when using the same set of colours.

Full colour palette exercise

◀ Use a dark warm brown to produce the initial drawing. With a compressed paper stump, vigorously blend the outline across the remaining surface to begin the suggestion of volume and shadow. Reinforce this now softened image with black line-work and the introduction of more detail. Generously fix this layer, using a spray fixative.

◀ Block on masses of colour, using directional strokes to shape the surface. With a broken piece of pastel stick work around, down and from edges, to sharply delineate them. Observe how the texture of the paper is discovered by the pastel strokes as they skate across the surface.

◀ Blending with a compressed paper stump pushes the pigment down into the lower reaches of the pastel paper. Note how the pastel dissipates toward the edges of the paper, allowing the colour of the paper to come through. This creates a vignette effect, with detail blurring toward the edges.

This exercise utilises a range of tints across a full range of colours and is completed in the same five stages as the limited tonal palette exercise:–

• Drawing out and shading
• Blocking in dark colour masses
• Successively applying colours working from dark to light tints
• Reworking with final layers of lightest tints of the colours
• Final white highlights, plus black accents

Warm brown pastel paper provides a harmonizing underlying surface for the full colour palette used to produce this study. The initial monochrome drawing needs to be heavily fixed, so that it will not adulterate the purity and intensity of the colours to follow.

The second layer of bright colour is blended strongly into the surface. This dulls the colour down, by spreading it more widely, allowing the under-colours to show through, but not mix.

However, when the final layer of colours are hatched and mixed on the surface, little blending is carried out. This allows the textures to develop and the colours to remain intense.

NOTE – THE FINISHED STUDY IS NOT FIXED, TO ENSURE IT RETAINS ITS BRILLIANCE OF COLOUR. THE PIECE THEREFORE NEEDS TO BE PROTECTED UNDER GLASS, IN A FRAME, AS SOON AS POSSIBLE.

Why do I need a special surface on which to paint in pastels?

The surface on which a pastel painting is created is almost as important as the quality of the pastel sticks being used. Choose the right surface and it will work with you, imbuing the work with an added dimension, through texture, colour and contrast.

It is important to understand how the choice of surface can work for, or against, the pastel medium.

SURFACE COLOUR

Since pastel is an opaque medium, it can be applied to a coloured surface. Although it is possible to completely cover the surface, any of the original surface colour that shows through will play an important role in the finished piece. The choice of surface colour is therefore crucial and requires careful consideration.

Surface colour could show through in two ways, both of which can be exploited to maximum effect.

Firstly, it may appear as little gaps between the pastel strokes. These accents can be of great significance, since they may be exploited to provide both a colour and value contrast.

For example, a blue grey sky has been painted. Tiny accents of an orange surface between the strokes would create a complementary contrast to the blue, making it appear brighter. The lighter the orange, the more intense the effect – the darker the orange, the lighter the blue grey would appear by contrast..

Secondly, surface colour can show through a thin, or thinned, stroke of pastel colour. Although pastels are opaque, it does not mean that they will necessarily obscure the surface or layer underlying them. Merely smearing a pastel stroke across the surface will render it semi-opaque, or even semi-transparent, depending on the amount of pastel present. The stroke of colour and the colour of the surface will then visually mix. Therefore, for example, a thin blue stroke applied over a red surface will appear purple.

Many types of coloured surface are available, from the cheaper sugar papers, through pastel paper to painted surfaces. The principal criteria to bear in mind - the permanency of the surface colour must be equal to the permanency of the pastels being used.

Sugar paper, for example, can come in very bright colours, which will provide wonderful contrasts for the overlaid pastel colours to work against. However, if the bright surface fades with time, so will the contrast and the painting will suffer.

Preparing one's own coloured underlying surface is an ideal way in which to manipulate the surface colour to ensure the desired end result. By underpainting with watercolour or acrylic paint, the composition can be based on the principle of providing a contrasting underlay, where dark, dull colours, or a bright complementary underpainting, provide a strong counterfoil. To achieve the strength of colour, especially with dark, dull colours, is not always easy with pastels. Artists' quality pastels are often too intense for underpainting.

Using watercolours or acrylics to paint this underlay makes it possible to not only create dull colours, but also to treat each area of the composition quite differently, if so required.

Being very fluid, watercolours will tend to swiftly soak into pastel paper, as would acrylics if applied in the form of thin washes. However, acrylics offer the added benefit of being able to be used more solidly and to build texture. They could also be used as a glue with which to adhere other materials to the surface, to provide other forms of structural texture over which to work. The possibilities are endless.

SURFACE THICKNESS

The thickness of the surface base should be borne in mind, as it can have a twofold effect on the work in hand.

The thinner the surface base, the more it is likely to flex and should it continue to do so while the pastel work remains unfixed, then the pastel is inclined to dislodge from the surface. To prevent this damage from occurring it is important to support thinner bases, such as pastel paper. Alternatively, a thicker surface base should be opted for, such as pastel board.

Thin surface bases will also allow irregularities from any supports beneath to be revealed in overlaid pastel strokes. To experience this for yourself, take a scrap of thin pastel paper and lay it on a heavily grained drawing board, or other support. Rub a pastel stick over the paper and note how the grain of the supporting board is revealed in the laid pastel strokes.

Whilst this effect could of course be exploited, it does have certain limitations which are more likely to be a nuisance. The solution is to ensure that the supporting surface beneath thin paper is as smooth as possible, or introduce an underlay between the paper and the supporting board.

SURFACE TEXTURE

Surface texture is by far the most important characteristic of all in respect to pastel painting. So much so, that it is specifically referred to as the 'tooth' of a surface. As this term implies, the tooth of the surface can grip and hold

on to the pastel pigment and the stronger or deeper the tooth, the more effective it is.

Were you to attempt to work with pastels on a smooth cartridge paper, the result would be disappointing. You would have to resort to 'pushing' the pastel into the surface and fibres of the paper, once applied, to ensure that some of it remains in place. While this would be fine for the most basic of pastel sketches, it is far from ideal to produce anything more worthwhile.

Pastel painting is about building up layers of colour, which requires a sturdy foundation that can only be offered by a surface with sufficient tooth.

Many a would-be pastel painter becomes frustrated as they desperately attempt to build light and depth into their work, only to fail miserably. It is natural to blame either the pastels or one's ability. In most cases, an appropriate surface is all that is required to overcome this hurdle.

Pastel painters have at their disposal a considerable range of surfaces specifically manufactured to work with dry pastels. However, there are even further dynamic possibilities, not only to create one's own surfaces, but to bring other media into play.

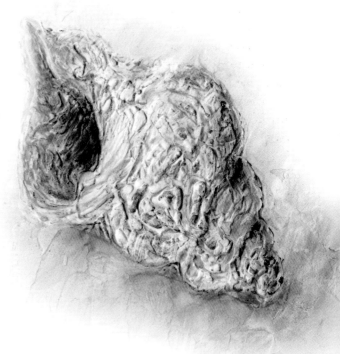

Understanding surfaces

Basic characteristics

For pastel painting it is essential to work on a surface that features a tooth. A smooth surface will simply not work, as it does not provide any grip to which the dry pastel can cling. Whilst a pastel stroke may appear to hold onto a smooth surface, the slightest vibration will shake it loose and the powdered pigment will fall away. Pastel papers manufactured with a tooth on their surface, or other surfaces specifically prepared for pastel painting, are the solution.

Basic types

PASTEL PAPER SURFACE FINISHES

There are many distinctively different pastel papers available, with each featuring its own particular finish and surface patina. In some, the patterning is uniform, while in others it is more amorphous. There are strong patterns and dainty patterns, coarse textures and fine. A plethora of choice and you may well find that one becomes a particular favourite, or your choice of surface can be matched to the nature of the subject being painted.

Whatever surface is selected, it will have a direct and dominant effect on the finish of the pastel painting. The surface quality will be brought into play in the final stages, when textures will be exploited as areas of light and highlight. At this point surface patterns will invariably become apparent.

It is therefore essential to experiment with different papers. You will undoubtedly experience disappointing results from time to time; this is part of the learning process and will serve to establish which papers are definitely not for you. The early days in trying out pastel painting is the best time to determine which papers and surfaces are more suited to you. There is nothing more frustrating than discovering a bad paper when your abilities at painting in pastels have improved to the stage that you would resent throwing the result in the dustbin!

PASTEL PAPER SURFACE COLOURS

Working on coloured pastel paper gives you the advantage of being able to exploit its colour as part of the composition. For maximum contrast, a yellow flower head is placed on a paper whose colour is the exact complementary purple of the yellow. When placed against a background colour within its own colour family, it is the value (darkness) of the background that provides the contrast. However, when placed against its own colour, it lacks vitality and the subtleties are lost, having neither a complementary contrast, nor a strong value against which to work. Choice of colour therefore also comes into play when determining what would work best for the desired end result.

PASTEL BOARDS

Do not be tempted to use other rough surfaces, such as sandpaper or glass-paper. Although these may at first glance appear ideal and will undoubtedly grip pastel, they are not suitable, being neither lightfast, nor acid-free. It is far better to consider pastel board with a surface not unlike that of glass-paper.

CAUTION – IN SOME INSTANCES THE GRANULES OF TEXTURE ARE ADHERED TO THE BASE OF THE PASTEL BOARD WITH GUM. THESE ARE NOT SUITABLE FOR USE WITH TECHNIQUES INVOLVING THE USE OF WET PAINT OR WETTING THE PASTEL. THE GUM WILL DISSOLVE AND THE SURFACE WILL DISINTEGRATE.

Alternatives

PREPARING YOUR OWN SURFACE TEXTURED

Start with a strong base, such as hardboard or plywood, which is less flexible than paper and therefore less likely to shake free the pastel layer. With hardboard, use the smooth surface uppermost, as the texture on the reverse is far too uniform, strong and rough. To remove the shiny surface and provide a surface tooth, use sandpaper to 'roughen' it up somewhat. You are now free to apply a texture of your making, such as a mix of acrylic medium (bonding agent) and sand (as shown). PVA or wood glues are equally suitable as bonding agents and can be mixed with a variety of texture producing materials. Alternatively artist products such as acrylic modelling paste would offer interesting possibilities.

PREPARING YOUR OWN SURFACE ENHANCED TOOTH

Using watercolour paints or acrylic paints to render the first layer, not only provides a contrasting background against which the pastel layers will shine. Either of these two media will also produce an enhanced tooth to grip the overlaying pastel. Not only can pastel papers be used for this technique, but also watercolour papers, with their inherent textures and weaves, not to mention acrylic surfaces and the like. The possibilities are endless.

Exercise for surfaces

Preparing your own surface – enhanced tooth

ARTSTRIPS©

Stretch pastel paper by briefly dipping through water. Allow excess water to run off. Stick to drawing board with gumstrip.

DRAWING - Since pastel is opaque the drawing can be done with a Rigger brush and Indian ink. Ink line can be easily seen against the colour.

Alternatively, use a felt-tip pen or brush pen. Mistakes with either can be easily covered with the pastel work to follow.

WATERCOLOUR UNDERPAINTING - Use dull watercolour mixes as underpainting to block in masses. Once completed…

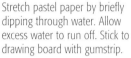

…return to apply darker accents. Do not worry about fast drying, hard watercolour edges. The pastel layers will soften these.

PASTELS FIRST STAGE – Begin with the darkest values of pastels in your colour palette.

Vary the pressure for different strengths of colour. The gum in the dry watercolour underpainting provides enhanced tooth that helps adhesion of the pastel layer.

This first layer can be blended, merging colours together and forcing them into the tooth of the surface.

Fixing can be carried out after these first layers. Surface tooth improves becomes slightly transparent, allowing more of the watercolour layer to show through.

Build the pastel layers from dark to light. Be sure you do not miss the range of middle values before arriving at the highlights.

By alternating layers of warm and cool colours you will also make the final colour mix more exciting to the eye.

TIP - Highlights which need to be applied with some pressure often spread beyond where they are required. Clean up edges with a sharp blade or knife.

A – Flecks of colour
These tiny highlights of white are so small that if made over complicated they will lose their impact. Apply them boldly and step back to see if they suggest what you want, rather than trying to capture every detail.

B – Strokes of colour
Strokes of gentle colour are so thin as to be almost transparent, allowing ink line and watercolour underpainting to softly show through. The effect can be increased by blending or fixing the strokes, either of which makes the strokes less opaque.

C – Dabs of colour
Small dabs of colour laid next to and over one another, move through many values, ending in white. Their close positioning and juxtaposition allows colours to shimmer out against one another. The shadow of the boat forms naturally where the value layering simply stops, at an early stage, thereby allowing more dark underpainting to show through.

When working with good quality pastels, such as the ultra soft Artists' Quality used in this exercise, to produce an effective dark underpainting layer can prove elusive. This is simply due to the fact that the darker the colour value of the pastel, the more pure pigment it holds. Although complementary pastel hues could be blended on the surface, it is often worthwhile resorting to darkening the surface before the pastel layers are applied.

The use of watercolour painting as the underpainting layer proves beneficial in several ways.

• First, it can darken and dull the surface, because such colour mixes are possible in fluid paint.

• Once dry, the surface is more stable than an underpainting completed in pastels. Not only does the inherent gum hold the fluid colour fast, it will also grip the subsequently applied layers of pastel more effectively.

• By applying different undercolours in different areas, the balance of the composition is well established before committing yourself to the pastel layers.

• Having no texture of its own, the watercolour layer does not detract from the opportunity to exploit the paper's own surface texture as the pastel strokes are subsequently laid.

Pastel paper must be stretched before watercolour is applied. Being very absorbent it needs little wetting to stretch and if overwet can tear as the stretching occurs. Furthermore, it must be stretched on a perfectly smooth board, as there is no possibility of padding the paper from beneath, once it is stretched.

However, having stretched the paper successfully and allowed the underpainting of watercolour to dry, it is a rewarding surface on which to work.

Exercise for surfaces Preparing your own surface – rough with texture

ACRYLIC MODELLING PASTES – comprise hard materials, ground down and mixed with acrylic medium. Transfer small amounts from tub to stay-wet palette as required.

ARTSTRIPS ©

Modelling paste can be applied with a variety of tools – brush, knife, finger etc.

Be sure to clean all tools thoroughly after applying the paste. It can set like concrete and will ruin anything not properly washed out.

TEXTURE SURFACE – use a painting knife like a trowel to scoop up paste from the palette. Spread evenly on the surface from one edge of the blade.

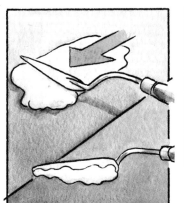

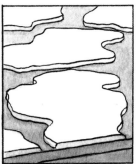

Resulting deposits tend to be flat with sharp edges.

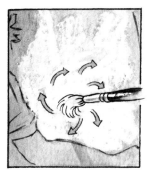

Use an oil painter's bristle brush to produce more vigorous surface texture…

…and the texture paste will become furrowed and striated.

Acrylics dry by evaporation. In spite of the heavy texture, the paste shrinks downward as it dries, losing bulk and depth.

Once dry, additional layers can be applied to create even more intriguing textures and deeper ridges.

In this exercise the ultimate surface tooth is built up as layers of acrylic texture/modelling paste, on a stretched sheet of grey pastel paper. The heavily textured surface of the shells is emulated by exploiting the nature of the paste. Slabs of paste are applied to provide a dynamic background foil against which the more organic rounded forms can work.

First the composition is defined with an outline pencil drawing, strengthened with an ink line, before applying the modelling paste. The texture paste is applied using a painting knife as well as a bristle brush. Directional brush-strokes are used to sculpt the structure of the shells, while the broad flat knife strokes suggest the flatter planes of the surface behind. Several layers have to be laid before all of the textures are adequately described.

A – Once the prepared surface is fully dry, small amounts of pastel are gently laid, using different colours to depict light or shadow.

B – These colours lie on the top of the texture work, until blended in with a compressed paper stump.

C – The lights of the surface are rediscovered by wiping off the pastel colours, where appropriate, with a kneadable putty rubber, to suggest lighter colours and highlights.

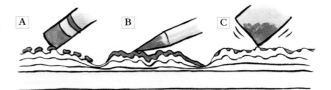

Discovering pastel qualities

To paint with soft pastels is to work with one of the most beautiful of all the media; one that offers a vast range of avenues to explore. Unlike paints, soft pastel sticks are almost entirely made of pure pigment, which sets their brilliance apart. Soft pastels can adhere not only to pastel papers but also to any surface that features a tooth, such as a watercolour layer, or acrylic underpainting.

When watercolour medium (gum solution) is added to pastels, the result is akin to an opaque watercolour, such as gouache. Little wonder that some watercolour artists carry the odd pastel colour to add to their paint or to use in dry form, for that added sparkle of intense colour.

This opens up a vast range of possibilities for anyone choosing to work with the pastel medium.

Having examined the varying degrees of softness of dry pastels in the basics section, we now move on to fully exploit their potential. The following exercise and stage-by-stage painting are intended to push the boundaries of the two varieties that form the basis of this book.

Dry sketching pastels are often underrated, but with judicious use of black and white in the applied layers, a good range of values is achieved. This allows the pastel painter to portray light falling across an object and to describe its form in space.

What better challenge than to paint white and yellow flowers, which form the subject of the exercise, as both feature a local colour that is very light in value. Learning how to reproduce the range of values

necessary to make the flowers appear three-dimensional will teach you much about the nature of light and how it may be captured.

As you explore the available varieties of sketching pastels, it will become obvious that even within this range of pastels, there is an array of different qualities. Although harder in nature than the Artists' Quality soft pastels, some sketching pastels contain more pigment and, or, gum than others. Pastels with higher pigment content are slightly costlier; however this is more than compensated for, as the resultant intense colour yields a far richer result.

Artists' Quality soft pastels offer a much wider range of values, which are maximised in the stage-by-stage painting to render a transparent object. Reflective and transparent surfaces condense light values from their environment and display them next to one another as part of their structure. By tackling a glass object, not only will much be learnt about values, but also which aspects within the composition should be kept soft-edged, even when depicting the hard surface and edges of glass.

CHOICE OF PASTELS

It may be that you discover the harder sketching pastels are all you need and really suit your method of working and temperament. However, when acquiring materials it is important to keep an open mind, break boundaries and not limit yourself. Therefore, although working with the better quality pastels might appear to be more expensive, they do offer the opportunity to acquire individual sticks. This makes it more affordable for you to experiment with different qualities and types of pastels, without burdening yourself with colours that could become redundant.

When moving on to Artists' Quality soft pastels it pays to extend your collection slowly. The range of colours and tints is vast and it is virtually impossible for anyone to acquire them all, quite apart from the fact that an entire collection would prove unworkable. Imagine having to search through hundreds of sticks during the course of a painting!

Pastels vary from one manufacturer to another, not only in type and degrees of softness, but in the colours and tints offered. This treasure trove of dazzling pigments can prove bewildering and it is all too easy to get carried away when making your selections.

Start off with a simple range of greys, or the limited palette of blues and browns featured in the basics section. Extend your palette of colours by moving into the primaries - red, yellow and blue. Then move on to the secondary colours - orange, purple and green. It may prove useful to have each of these colours in a warm and a cool bias, to allow for a greater degree of colour temperature control.

Whatever the starting point, it soon becomes obvious to every artist that they are developing a palette of colours which meets their particular requirements. Be discriminating from the outset and you too will slowly build your own unique range of preferred types, colours and tints.

STORING PASTELS

Good working practice pays dividends when using pastels.

• They need to be kept in order and intact, both indoors and during transport.

• They need to be kept as clean as possible, in order that individual hues and tints can be easily and quickly identified as you work.

Pastels therefore need to be firmly stored and every stick needs to be kept separate from the others.

Sharpen one end of sketching pastel using large pencil sharpener or sharp blade.

Explore different ways of making line with pastel stick. (Top) edge. (Middle) point, side on. (Bottom) drawn point.

Explore different ways of making broad strokes. (Top) whole pastel. (Middle) broken piece. (Bottom) sharpened shoulder.

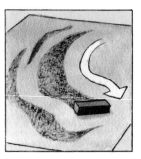

Explore descriptive qualities of pastels. With small pastel piece apply spontaneous strokes, at different pressures.

SKETCHING OUT – Sketch out basic shapes of flower heads (reversible cups and saucer shapes). Central stem is also line of symmetry.

Basic shapes form skeleton on which to help you draw in simplified structure of petals in another colour.

BLENDING COLOUR – Blend and soften broad areas of background between petals. [Either flat pastel shaper as shown, or use compressed paper stump]

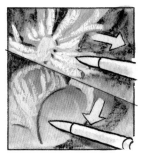

Use rounder pastel shaper, or compressed paper stump to soften and shape petals. Follow direction of strokes for linear petals (top), or across strokes to effect more rounded forms (bottom).

IMPORTANT – Continuously wipe blenders clean on absorbent paper towels. Otherwise blenders will begin to transfer colour, rather than blend previously deposited pastel.

DETAILING – Black pastel contrasts produce dramatic accents. These tend to be austere and dull. However…

…when overlaid with coloured pigment [brown], accents will regain their richness while also retaining a dark value.

Sharp whites against strong darks create strong contrasts, which are essential for suggesting the effects of lights.

Exercise

This exercise uses sketching pastels combined with blenders, to achieve a painterly feel. The dainty subject also demonstrates that the use of sketching pastels need not be as clumsy as some would expect.

STEP 1 – For this exercise, try some square sketching pastels, working on pastel paper. Here, the flowers were made a little larger than life in order that their structures could be explored. Lightly sketch in the basic structure, working mostly in light blue (which can be easily overlaid). Tighter drawing could be carried out with more pressure, using the same colour (daisies) or in a second colour (buttercup) for definition. First, block in the background, or negative shapes, 'nibbling' into the flowers to begin to describe their silhouette. Block in the petals and stems, using simple, but bold, strokes of colour.

STEP 2 – Strengthen and redraw negative shapes around the subject, using a darker brown. Yellow is employed liberally on flower heads, centres and stems. This invokes the feel of sunlight, which is naturally yellow. Note how reshaping of the petals continues in the buttercup. A white pastel, drawn down the daisy petals with varied pressure begins the final highlights. Note how undercolour still shows through, depending on pressure used. A light green applied on the light yellow of the stems, re-introduces the local colour.

STEP 3 – Since, the palette of colours in this type of pastel is limited, the introduction of black is essential to achieve maximum contrasts. Cover black with a second colour and any problems of dullness are removed.

A sharpened pastel produces all the detail required, but, if you wish, you could switch to Pastel Pencils at this stage. These are usually available in matching colours and are very useful for those who love lots of detail.

Here however, they are not used, as the flowers are sufficiently large to render with the sharpened pastel point – note how even the fuzz under the petals of the buttercups is achieved. For the finishing touch, add soft blue reflected highlights to the stem, leaving them less finished than the flowers, so as not to detract from the latter.

Stage-by-stage

The aim of this study is to explore the layering attributes of Artists' Quality soft pastels and to discover just what degree of contrast is available as several layers of pastel are overlaid.

Begin on a piece of medium value pastel paper. Choose a colour that will harmonize with the underpainting colours to be applied.

STAGE 1
DRAWING AND UNDERPAINTING BASE LAYER

Step 1 - Break off a piece of the darkest brown pastel and use an edge to draw in the main silhouette. Turn the piece in your fingers to present it side-on and block in some very gentle shading to render the main areas of dark, so that you achieve the first suggestion of solidity. You are aiming for a vignette effect, where the drawing fades at the edge. When blocking in the background therefore, note that it does not reach the paper edges, but dissipates into a general rounded form.

Step 2 – With a compressed paper stump, push and smear the pastel into and over the paper tooth. You can be quite aggressive with the shaded areas, allowing them to migrate further toward the edge of the paper. This will help the progression of the vignette effect. With more important lines of drawing, the blender must travel along the same direction as the strokes were laid. This is necessary to keep lines fixed in position, although their depth of colour will be solidified.

To prevent this dark, underpainting base layer from mixing with subsequent layers of pastel, the surface of the work can now be fixed quite heavily.

STAGE 2 – BLOCKING IN COLOUR

Mid to dark value colours are now blocked on throughout the painting. First, broadly stroke in the background with a dull green. Although dull, being an opposite colour temperature to the brown beneath, the green will appear full of colour. This colour is carried through the neck of the decanter and the body of the glass. Transparent objects allow the colours behind them to show through. They also pick up accents and lights from other parts of the environment and closely juxtapose them to create strong contrasts.

Since these are only the first colours to bleed through the glass from behind, the overall effect remains soft and indistinct.

Although the liquid in the decanter is a different, much warmer hue, it is very close in value to the colour behind it. In other words, the light has the same strength as it penetrates the glass of the decanter, but it is bestowed with another colour by the liquid within.

Heavy blending is now required, the direction of the blend following the forms of the glass. Imagine yourself fashioning these same shapes in wood. Use the blender to sculpt the shape, as if it were a chisel, following the contours and structure of the object. Blending of the background can be much looser, but do not lose the definition of the shadows. Although the shadows are soft, they do hold the objects together within the composition. The surface can now be gently fixed.

To achieve the strokes and line-work, you need to use a small section of the pastel stick. Using the whole length is clumsy and allows only the tip to be presented to the paper surface. By using a smaller piece, the sharp broken end can be used for line and the side for wider brush-like strokes.

TO SNAP OFF DESIRED LENGTH OF PASTEL PIECE
Run your fingernail around the point at which the pastel length is to be snapped off.

This forms a light groove and the gentlest of pressure is all that is required to snap the length off at this point.

Immediately return the original pastel stick to its usual storage place, to ensure it can be easily located when required in the future.

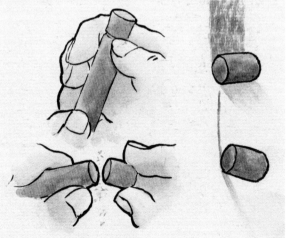

NOTE – TO PREVENT DAMAGE TO YOUR PAINTING – DO THIS OVER A SCRAP PIECE OF PAPER SO THAT CRUMBS OF PASTEL DO NOT SOIL YOUR WORK, OR SURROUNDING WORK SURFACE.

Stage-by-stage

STAGE 3 – FIRST LAYER

To fully capture the reflectivity of the glass surface, accents (small dark areas) will be as important as highlights. Use a very dark brown, or a black, to redraw the silhouette of both decanter and glass. It is important however to keep this line-work irregular. In some places it is very thick, whilst in others it virtually disappears.

These accents are now carried inside the objects. Directional strokes of the dark accent colours are used within the glass stopper and neck of the decanter, to more fully describe their internal structures and facets. Working from the top downward (to prevent damage to the pastel surface through smudging), draw in the cut glass pattern around the base of the decanter.

A mid-value blue-green is now played around the base of both the decanter and the glass - thus sharpening some of their silhouette edges and those of some parts of the shadow.

Use the same pastel judiciously, down the left hand side of the glass. At the top – where a hint of light in the decanter stops at the glass edge, gently separating the two objects. Below – it should follow the curved edge of the glass, where it stands in front of the decanter body.

Note how the surface beneath decanter and glass receives cool light. This suggests that the ambient light is falling only on this surface. It misses the area behind the two glass objects, which remain dark. As a consequence, the two surfaces appear to be distinctly differently orientated to the light – one seeming to be flat, the other upright.

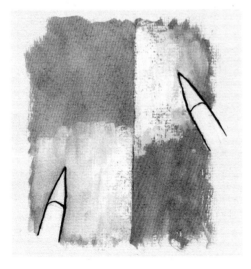

Silhouette edges of objects such as glass often need to be reinforced by painting the negative space up against them, rather than drawing the edge of the object as line. In this diagram you can imagine the 'edge' running down the centre becomes stronger as the lighter blue pastel is blocked right up against it. At the top, this pastel is deposited against the right hand of the 'edge'. Below it is blocked up to the left hand of the 'edge'. Moving down this 'edge' it now reads as dark against light, at the top and light against dark, at the bottom.

This is the basis of a technique know as counterchange – where the maximum contrast of value along an edge is employed.

The outer areas of the pastel (away from the edge), need to be softened into the background, so that they too do not read as being sharp-edged. Essentially, the only part of the pastel deposit that should remain sharp is that up against the edge that is being reinforced. Look at the glass in this stage of the painting and let your eye take a journey around its silhouette edge, to see how this works in practice.

STAGE 4 – SECOND LAYER

Considerable patience is required at this stage, to hold firmly within the mid-lights. Introduce the highlights too soon and the finished result will suffer.

Apply touches of warm blue throughout the glass, which will bring it forward - even though the blue is the same value as the background. This is a subtle use of colour temperature differences. Warm colours always appear to stand in front of cool colours. This theory is one of the mainstays of aerial perspective, which would normally be associated with landscape painting. By bringing the concept of aerial perspective into the confines of a still-life, our eyes are fooled into believing that the composition has depth, through exploiting colour temperature variation. These colours do exist, but it helps if you know what you are looking for, otherwise their subtleties could be missed.

Add mid-lights to the interior of the glass objects and to the ground. Note how much variety has been achieved in the strokes. Those on the ground are broad and generous. Within the glass and decanter, however, the strokes become much smaller and are used to depict the shards of light that are captured by the cut glass surface on the decanter. Also note how the background blue-green is now introduced into the decanter, where it appears as touches of light picked up by the cut glass in front of the surface of the liquid.

Blending is still effective if used gently at the edges of newly laid areas – glass bases and interiors.

Artists' Quality soft pastels are perfectly adapted for providing you with the means to build up several layers, in order that you can progressively move toward the highlights. However, there is a potential problem, for our eyes spend most of their time moving around the brighter lit areas of a scene, or parts of an object, especially picking out the highlights. Glass is a perfect example of this and we all react to and enjoy those rich lights inside glass, not to mention the sparkling highlights that describe its surface. We are all keen to get on to that part of the painting.

However, hard, bright highlights cannot work unless they are seen against the contrast of soft dull shadow areas and these need to be established first. It is important to learn to blank out the succulent highlights and to look below the surface lights to the soft dark colours that lie beneath.

The secret is to slowly move from the darks, through a succession of mid values that account for the majority of the painting.

Try this exercise out for yourself to learn how gradual colour build up is more effective. Squint your eyes and look at the top row of five colours, which represent the colours used on the glass – they only gradually become lighter. Move to the bottom row of three colours, where the middle values are missing and the highlight colour will not read as effectively.

Stage-by-stage

STAGE 5 – SECOND LAYER

Lighter blues are now peppered around the background and the surface
on which the decanter and glass stand. To the top right they are used to
reclaim the shape of the backlight, envisaged in the earliest stages, but
since lost into a more solid block. Note how directional these strokes
have now become. Although both the ground and the backdrop are
treated to the same colour of stroke, the change of direction in their
application is used to suggest that they lie at differing angles to the light.

The light blues are now used to bolster the contrast at the outside
edges of the glass. Let your eye travel around these silhouettes to
observe the variations of contrast used. For example, a solid light blue
down the left hand side of the decanter becomes broken into strokes
as your gaze moves upwards. Moving down, the contrast at the edge is
picked up by a mid blue within the glass itself. Move to the top rim of
the glass and you will discover that the edge is a line drawn with the
edge of the same light blue pastel. Move down the right hand side of
the glass and this fine line dissolves into a mid blue.

Inside the glass objects the light blue is used to describe the
lie of the glass surface. Lights from all about are reflected around the shiny surface and contrast
against the darks that have been painstakingly evolved. This is the effect you are aiming for, but
again, be patient. Reserve your light values and whites for the final highlights that follow.

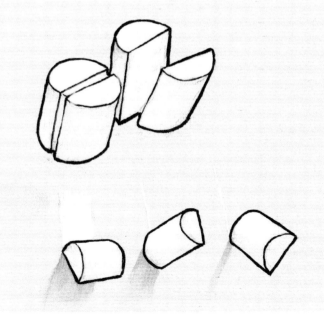

At this stage of the painting you need smaller strokes
and finer detail, just as you would with paint and brush.
The small pastel pieces, broken from the larger sticks, need
to be snapped again, following the same procedure as
previously used. These not only provide you will smaller
pieces for more narrow strokes, but also a set of renewed
sharp edges for line-work and detail.

As these smaller pieces are used - turn them in your
fingers to present either a sharp edge or point to the
surface. Slowly the shapes of these smaller pieces will
change as they wear down. However, do not discard them,
for they remain useful, even as the smallest of shards.
It may sound parsimonious to use such little pieces, but
they really are tremendously useful and more importantly,
these small shards achieve marks which the larger pieces
simply cannot provide. It is even possible to wedge a tiny
piece underneath a fingernail and draw with that!

STAGE 6 – FINISHING TOUCHES

All your patience will now pay off, as you approach the
highlights. Use your lightest orange within the body of
the glass decanter, where the light shines through the
amber liquid. These will be so exciting to apply that
you must show restraint and not overdo them. Step
back frequently, both physically and mentally, to check
their progress.

Finally – the pure white highlights. Again, note their
irregularity, for example, the rim of the glass. The
highlight comes and goes as it travels around the
circumference. Should you find yourself being a little
heavy handed when applying this fine edge, simply
scrape away any excess with an erasing knife.

NOTE – YOU MAY NEED TO BREAK THE WHITE PASTEL SEVERAL TIMES INTO
SMALLER AND SMALLER PIECES TO ENSURE ENOUGH SHARP EDGES FOR SUCH
DETAIL.

Common problems

Solution

Kneadable putty rubbers are best suited for the job, but they really need to be understood to get the best out of them. As the name implies, the rubber is soft and kneadable. The degree of softness can vary across the various makes. These rubbers need to be stored away from direct contact with the air, as they will deteriorate. Wrap them in plastic food wrap or keep them in a box with a closely fitting lid. To save on wastage, cut off a smaller piece to work with, keeping the original safely stored away.

As the rubber becomes dirty with pastel do not be tempted to pull off the soiled area and discard it. Instead, fold the soiled area inwards, to the middle of the rubber, which will reveal a clean area with which to continue working. Eventually the piece being used will need replacing, but not until it actually begins to deposit more colour than is removed.

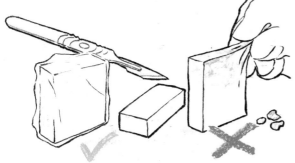

Being kneadable, the putty rubber can be shaped to be used as a tool in its own right.

For instance, when manipulated into a wedge shape, the rubber is very effective in lifting off a line of colour (Fig A), or a stroke (Fig B).

Fig C – Dabbing the pastel surface gently lifts colour gradually, over a more general, amorphous area.

The pliability of the putty rubber ensures that not only does it lift the pastel well, but it is not likely to damage the generally fragile surface of the pastel paper itself.

The possibilities are quite wide-ranging, proving that a kneadable putty rubber can be exploited as an invaluable tool, alongside the pastels and blenders which form the basic painting kit for pastel painters.

As with all painting tools, there are different makes, all of which possess different characteristics. It is a matter of personal choice as to which will suit best and it is important to try these out to determine which that will be.

TIP:

Harder varieties of kneadable putty rubber can be softened by holding them in the palm of the hand, while working, so that they warm and soften.

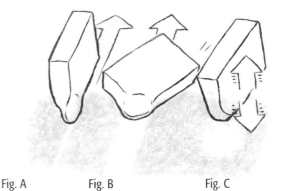

Fig. A   Fig. B   Fig. C

Common problems

FIXING PASTEL WORK

Fixative can do as much harm as good if it is improperly used. Having built up layers of colour and achieved both softness and exciting highlights, it is exceedingly disappointing to destroy their effectiveness in an attempt to preserve them by using fixative.

Reason

As fixative, by necessity, gently dissolves the pigment in order to bind it together and to the surface, some of the subtlety of the pastel work will be lost.

To experience this and see the resultant effect, take a discarded practice pastel sketch and mask a small area with a piece of paper. Use spray fixative to heavily fix the remaining areas of the sketch. Remove the mask and note the changes that have occurred.

Uses

Because fixing dulls down applied pastel work, many artists will only fix early layers, allowing the top layers of pastel to depend on the tooth of the surface, to which they are being applied, to hold them fast. It is a matter of personal choice as to which layers to fix, something that can be determined after having experimented with various options.

However, fixing can also be used to correct an overly light layer. Should the layering become too light, too soon, fixative can be used to intentionally dull it down. Not only will the colour values merge, but the surface will also be stabilized to allow for further work with lights and highlights.

ARTSTRIPS ©

Fixative in liquid (top) or aerosol form (bottom) is essential for fixing the early stage of a pastel painting. NOTE – the liquid form requires a diffuser

Take care not to allow large droplets to fall on the surface, as they can damage the fragile pastel. More likely with liquid form.

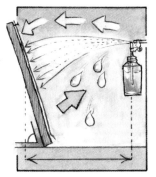

Fix work to tilted board. Keep at least 50cm (18″) away for spraying. This ensures fixative hits the surface gently as a mist.

Continue spray beyond confines of painting for even coverage. Three fine layers of fixative are better than one, over-heavy spraying.

TIP:

If you can see the fixative hitting the pastel, you are using too much or are too close.

Exploiting wet and dry blending

The ability to blend soft pastels equips the pastel painter with a far greater range of techniques and effects than would otherwise be possible if using pastel strokes alone. Not only can blending be used to maximum effect as a method of thinly spreading pastels, it proves equally indispensable when working with heavier applications of pastel.

VARIOUS BLENDING TOOLS can be used to thinly spread applied pastels and the degree to which the layers intermix depends on three factors.

First - the stability of the underlays. The more the underlays are fixed, the less they will impinge on overlaid pastel colours.

Second – the pressure exerted to overlay colours. The greater the pressure employed, the better the coverage, since more pigment will be deposited.

Third – the choice of blending tool. Different types of blending tool will yield diverse results, directly affecting the spread and therefore, how the colours mix. Blending with a rolled paper wiper will differ quite substantially from doing so with a brush, be the brush either wet or dry.

All of these changeable and subtle characteristics furnish the pastel painter with a repertoire of marks and effects at his or her fingertips.

Having explored the advantages of thinly blending pastels to produce an effect not unlike that of the line and wash technique in watercolour painting, the exercise and tutorial in this section move up a level.

Leaving behind the confines of line, it is the pastel itself that is manipulated to define shapes and suggest light and volume.

Applied more heavily, the opacity of this medium can be fully exploited and a thick layer will entirely blanket whatever lies beneath. However, if used more frugally, the undercolours and textures beneath can be allowed to show through, to a greater or lesser degree.

To fully comprehend these techniques, it is essential to experience them through application and use, since it is the feel of the pastels that is every bit as important.

PAINTING WITH BLENDERS AND PASTELS
Although the concept of turning pastel into a wet medium may appear to belong within the confines of mixed media, it does not. Instead, this technique is used in the following exercise and stage-by-stage painting to explore the precise nature of pastels.

Pastels are opaque and as with all opaque media, they offer the pastel painter the bonus of being able to work in layers, building up from dark to light. In other words, pastels can blanket and the degree of cover is determined by the manner in which it is spread, once applied to the surface.

In its raw form, it is a dry medium. As such, it lies on the surface of the surface and is totally dependant on the tooth or texture of that surface to hold it fast. There are ways in which the surface grip can be improved and strengthened.

One of which is to apply a fixative; which is, in essence, a gum that is evenly sprayed across the entire surface. For a few moments the surface becomes wet, causing the pigments, lying side by side, or over each other, to meld and bind together. The pastel colours take on some of the attributes of paint. As they dry, the gum hardens and like glue, holds the pigments together, whilst also binding them to the surface.

Fixing is however rather too general, since it is applied across the whole painting. It does nothing more than solidify the surface and bind the colour together.

By adding a gum selectively, the painter can, however, introduce this process as part of the build up of layers and the structure of the drawing. This requires the application of a gum medium.

Watercolour medium is composed of gum Arabic and water, with a little preservative added. Gum Arabic comes in either liquid form or as water-soluble crystals and is in fact the base medium within a tube of watercolour paint, which delivers a transparent paint. However, when watercolour medium is used in conjunction with pastels, the resultant mix is much more opaque.

Fixative and watercolour medium dull pastel colours as the pigments become relatively more transparent, as well as adhering them more strongly to the surface. Both of these qualities can be harnessed to the benefit of the painter.

Dulling colours in early stages can prevent colour becoming too bright too soon, a common problem. Fixing the colours on the surface allows more layers of pastel to be applied and built up.

Therefore, although you will be working with dry pastel pigment for these techniques, the concept of initially fixing and manipulating it on the surface requires the use of wet blending, which allows for the introduction of brushes into your repertoire.

Once the initial layers have been established, the overlaid colours thereafter are built up in dry pastel form. Blending at these stages is carried out with the appropriate tools, such as compressed paper stumps and rolled paper wipers.

It is important that the final layers of a pastel painting are not fixed, since it is essential that lights and highlights retain their full intensity and light value. The more gum utilised in underlying layers, the easier these highlights will be to apply.

Opaque pastel colour delivers intense highlights, which is occasionally used by watercolorists to add a final sparkle to their transparent pigments.

For the pastel painter, it is the final delight offered by this medium, the moment worth waiting for. All of the soft blending and manipulation in underlying layers is now lit with a sharp focussed highlight and the painting is complete.

NOTE – WHEN BLENDING WET OR DRY, DUE CONSIDERATION NEEDS TO BE GIVEN TO THE DIRECTION IN WHICH THE BLENDS ARE TO BE CARRIED OUT. THIS TOO CAN BECOME AN IMPORTANT ASPECT IN DICTATING THE NATURE OF THE FINISHED PIECE. DIRECTIONAL BLENDING CAN FOR INSTANCE, BE MADE TO SUGGEST VOLUME AND/ OR MOVEMENT.

Excercise

WATERCOLOUR PAINT comprises pigment dissolved with gum (the glue that sticks the pigment to the surface). Watercolour paint is generally transparent.

SOFT DRY PASTEL STICKS comprise pigments compressed together and fixed with minimal quantity of gum. Added white pigment makes them opaque.

WATERCOLOUR MEDIUM is a solution containing gum – the same base glue, or medium, found in watercolour paint.

Mixed with watercolour it adds strength and depth. Added to pastel it dissolves pigment, increasing fluidity, strength and coverage.

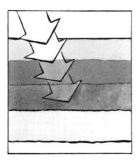

LAYERS OF TRANSPARENT WATERCOLOUR PAINT progressively absorb more light.

Therefore, when consistently overlaid, layers will at some point, whether by accident or by design, become dull.

LAYERS OF OPAQUE PASTEL however reflect pure colour from their surface.

Layers can therefore be overlaid, building from dark to light.

DISSOLVING/WET BLENDING SOFT DRY PASTELS - Adding water dissolves pastel pigment, making it easy to spread.

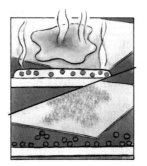

Once water has evaporated off, the pigment is left as a powder, which is vulnerable to damage.

Adding a fluid gum medium to the water turns the pastel pigment into paint on the surface.

Once water has evaporated off, the pigment is fixed to the surface by the gum.
NOTE – THE PAINT IS SLIGHTLY DULLER THAN THE PURE PASTEL PIGMENT.

Wet brush and rolled paper wiper blending

The paper chosen for this exercise features a particularly strong honeycomb texture, which directly and powerfully affects the quality of the strokes throughout the painting. Certainly, the first dark green layer is heavily disturbed by this surface grain. Although this quality may appeal, the underpainting layer often works better if it is slightly more solid in appearance. To achieve this, the pastel could be blended down into the deeper layers of the paper surface, using a compressed paper stump.

However, for this study, wet brush blending is used to render the underpainting layer. Apply the first dark green layer of pastel. Prepare a mix comprising equal quantities of water and watercolour medium. With a large brush, brush some of this mix over the strokes of dry pastel. This will carry the colour into the lower reaches of the paper surface. It also allows you to use the tip of the brush to carry some colour to the silhouette edge, to suggest smaller groupings of leaf and some branches.

Leave this layer to dry thoroughly, before continuing to build pastel colours from mid-values to lights. Move to a lighter cool green for the shadows and a warm yellow-green for the sunlight. Apply to tree leaf masses and grass and blend gently with a rolled paper wiper.

Use a mid-orange to begin the sunlight accents which catch the back of the trunk.

Blending ceases at this point, when the final highlights are applied. These comprise of a lighter yellow-green applied to the tree and grass, with a bright yellow used to add that final sparkle of sunlight to the trunk.

Less blended highlight areas display the texture of the paper surface to the best effect. Here you can see the honeycomb pattern quite clearly. If such a distinct texture does not appeal opt for a different paper

Here the dark honeycomb pattern is the pastel remaining from the first wet blended layer. It's presence indicates that the brushing was very gentle, only moving enough pigment to fill in the gap. It is however very stable being fixed by the drying of the gum in the applied solution.

Stage-by-stage
Wet brush and compressed paper stump blending

This study of a yellow rose is completed on a mid-toned pastel paper. To ensure the richness of colours necessary in the darks at the base of the petals the surface is first to be given a layer of dark watercolour. When using a thin paper such as this on which to apply a water-based underpainting, it is inevitable that cockling or buckling of the surface will occur. A cockled surface will not accept the pastel smoothly and it is therefore essential to stretch the paper. Furthermore, the paper must be stretched on a smooth and even drawing board, since it will not be possible to underlay the paper with newspaper or card once it is stretched.

NOTE – THIS IS ALWAYS A THOUGHT-PROVOKING STAGE, BUT WITHOUT THESE DULL DARK COLOURS, THERE WILL BE NO CONTRAST FOR THE BRIGHT, LIGHT COLOURS THAT FOLLOW.

STAGE 1 – DRAWING AND UNDERPAINTING BASE LAYER

Step 1 – Initial drawing out
The initial drawing can be carried out either before stretching the paper, or once stretched. Allow the paper to thoroughly dry before starting to work on it. As thin pastel paper is not strong, working on it whilst still wet can cause damage and in some cases could also lead to tearing.

Step 2 – Watercolour underpainting
Blocking in colour masses
Be bold in applying the watercolour strokes. Paint them wet-on-dry and do not worry about any hard edges that may occur, as these will disappear under the opaque pastel pigment. The background is to eventually fade away at the edges as a vignette. At this stage however concentrate on achieving a shape behind the flower head that will enhance the balance of the composition.

Keep the colour mixes dark and dull, using the complementary mixes to dull down this underpainting. Applying coloured greys ensures that the rich, pure pastel strokes will sing out as they are overlaid.

Pastel paper is not made for painting, so do not worry that it dries fast. Get the structure of the flower right, even if you have to make several corrections. The pastel layers to come will easily disguise any changes.

STAGE 2 – UNDERPAINTING
BLOCKING IN PASTEL COLOUR

The paper must be thoroughly dry before proceeding with any pastel work. You will now discover that the underlying painted areas make a rewarding surface on which to work. The gum in the paint makes it more physically receptive to the pastel pigment. Pastel colours against the dull greys beneath really shine out, but do not be alarmed by their clarity. Soon they will be muted as they are dissolved and spread across the flower petals. These colours, bright as they appear now, will also form the underpainting, as they intermingle with the paint beneath.

The background is to remain as dark coloured greys and therefore needs careful manipulation.

Warm colours are laid over cool and vice versa, so that, although dark, the background retains its visual excitement. It must also provide a stimulating tonal contrast for the flower head.

Do not fuss with detail at this stage. Make the most of bold pastel strokes, applied edge-on to the paper. Use the pastel point sparingly for line or fine strokes along the edge of a petal, to begin to suggest the direction of the light source.

DIRECTIONAL PASTEL STROKES - Directional strokes of pastel suggest volume and shape. In this diagram the pastel piece is applied edge-on and the amount of pigment deposited is dependent on the pressure applied when making the stroke. Areas of gentle application naturally suggest shadow. Heavier pressure and more pigment is applied to lights and highlights. In this way you are not just making use of the pastel colour, but also bringing the paper colour beneath into play. Carefully read each petal to decide on the direction in which the pastel stroke should be applied and vary the pressure to further suggest volume.

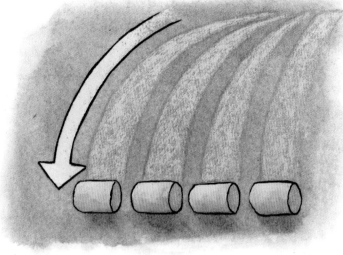

Stage-by-stage

STAGE 3 – UNDERPAINTING
DISSOLVING/WET BLENDING PASTEL COLOUR

Prepare a mix with equal quantities of water and watercolour medium. Use a medium to large watercolour brush, to stroke some of this mix over the dry pastel. This will spread the pigment and merge the pastel colours together. After the water evaporates off, the remaining gum fixes the pigment to the surface, thus effectively creating opaque watercolour paint on the paper surface. Once dry, the resultant surface will be much more stable for building layers of pastel. However, as well as binding the pigment, the gum inevitably dulls the colour down somewhat. During the early stages this can prove quite an advantage, since it mutes the colours to create a more acceptable underpainting.

These brush-strokes should be directional, following the structure of the petals. In doing this, you will discover how they interact with one another, preparing you for the build up of the lighter pastel colours.

The purpose of this layer is to use the brush to merge the colours on the surface, not to paint with the brush. To this end, use the gentlest of pressure on the brush as it moves over the petals. The bright, light colours will dissipate, but do not despair, as you have now established a solid, soft focussed, mid-value layer on which to build back towards light.

NOTE – THE BRUSH WILL PICK UP COLOUR AS IT TRAVELS ACROSS THE PETALS AND CAN SOON BEGIN TO TRANSFER THIS COLOUR. IT MUST THEREFORE BE CLEANED FREQUENTLY TO PREVENT THIS FROM HAPPENING AND WILL, AS A RESULT, ALSO NEED TO BE RELOADED WITH THE WATERCOLOUR MEDIUM/WATER MIX.

TIP:
There are some instances where transferring colour picked up by the brush could be utilised as a technique in its own right (top right hand background area).

DIRECTIONAL BRUSH-STROKES – A solution of watercolour medium and water is brushed onto the pastel strokes using a medium to large brush. The pigment granules are blended together by the wet brush. Inevitably some of the intensity of pastel is lost. However, by ensuring the strokes of the brush respond to the direction in which the pastel was applied, the structure of the subject will be retained. The gum also solidifies the surface, making it more responsive to the addition of further layers of pastel.

STAGE 4 – MID-VALUES
PASTEL LAYER

Allow the surface to dry thoroughly before blocking on the mid-value colours. At this stage it is necessary to hold back as long as possible from applying highlights. It is very tempting to rush into these, as they would look wonderful against the soft, dull colour that you have been at pains to create. However, the more gradually you build towards light, the more successful the end result.

Progressively work towards lighter and lighter values of colour, wiping and blending the colours as you go. The paper texture now begins to make itself known, once more – blend to soften where necessary. Different values of a colour are blended together along the edges where they meet, to create soft gradations from dark to light. Take care that overlaid colours are not over-heavy.

Dark accents left between petals are as important as the highlights. Shadows should be soft and you therefore do not want to have to revisit these accents to redraw them. Manage to always work lighter and lighter and any darks left behind will be naturally soft-focussed.

Although the flower is progressing nicely at this stage, the vignette edges of the background will have become too dominant and will therefore need to be knocked back in the final stage.

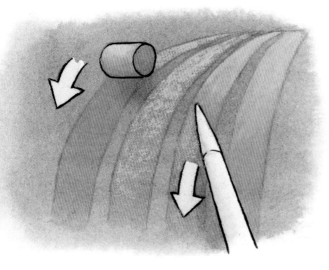

DIRECTIONAL BLENDING WITH ROLLED PAPER WIPER – Further directional pastel strokes are applied over previously established strokes, following their existing pattern. This will effectively reinforce the contrasts and highlights of those strokes. The gum beneath serves to make the surface really responsive to pressure variations, which takes on the soft qualities associated with pastel. Use a rolled paper wiper to consolidate and blend the dry pastel pigment, changing and softening the nature of the texture and volume. A succession of pastel strokes and blends can be overlaid until the required strength and hue of colour has been achieved.

NOTE – THE ROLLED PAPER WIPER ALSO FOLLOWS THE DIRECTIONAL NATURE OF THE ESTABLISHED UNDERPAINTED STROKES.

▲ Within the rose head, colour values run across the full range, from dark accents to white highlights. Although our eyes tend to fix on either of these extremes, the suggestion of light and volume is only achieved through the application of gently graduating mid-values. It is essential to exercise patience in building and blending these gradated colours.

NOTE – THE WARM, INTENSE ORANGES IN THE DEPTHS OF THE PETALS

▲ The rose stem is a perfect example of how the layers work together. At the base, the dark undercolours of the stem are soft and dissolve into the background. Conversely, the highlights at the top focus our attention immediately.

NOTE – NEGATIVELY PAINTED GREY STROKE IN THE BACKGROUND (BOTTOM RIGHT), WHICH EMPHASISES THE STEM EDGE [DARK AGAINST LIGHT]. WHILST THE STEM APPEARS LIGHT AGAINST DARK AT THE TOP LEFT. THIS IS USE OF COUNTERCHANGE TO GREAT EFFECT.

► Blocking out the clumsy shape and sharp edge of the background grey-green is achieved by using a mid grey. Squint your eyes and observe that although this is a different colour to the paper, it has the same value. Because we visually respond to value rather than colour, the edge appears to dissolve as the values merge.

STAGE 5 – FINAL LAYER

All your patience will now pay dividends as you work up to the sharp focus of the highlights. These final highlights can be achieved with a white pastel and will work on any coloured area, providing the values have been gradually built up from dark to light. Should the values have not been progressively applied, the whites will stand apart from the colours on which they have placed and the painting will take on the appearance of being speckled with snow. To correct this problem wherever necessary, is relatively simple. Return to the affected area or stroke and build up the required graduation of mid-values.

On the other hand, you may find that your painting was too light at the end of the previous layer to benefit from the addition of these final highlights.

To rectify this, gently spray the surface with fixative before starting the final layer – this will darken down the overall values. On contact with the surface, the damp fixative mist moistens the pastel grains, which welds them together and mixes the colours. Darker colour from beneath mix with the lighter colours on the top layer and their values darken.

CAUTION - IT IS EASY TO APPLY THE FIXATIVE TOO HEAVILY, WHICH COULD RESULT IN THE LOSS OF SOME OF THE SUBTLE MID-VALUES. SHOULD THIS HAPPEN THE MID-VALUES WILL NEED TO BE REAPPLIED.

TIP:

A white highlight may become too large, usually as a consequence of the pressure required to apply it, causing the white pastel to spread - this is easily corrected.

Use the curved blade of an erasing knife to cut these highlights down to the exact proportions required.

Common problems

ROLLED PAPER WIPERS

Rolled paper wipers are required for blending and, for whatever reason; there aren't any in your painting kit. This would not only prove frustrating, it could seriously affect the outcome of your painting.

Solution

Not only will making your own save the day, but there are other benefits, such as being able to produce a selection for use with specific colours, not to mention the cost saving.

A rolled paper wiper, as its name implies, is paper rolled to produce a blending tool. Using up scraps of paper will prove ideal. Sugar paper, pastel paper, blotting paper, whatever is to hand. Different papers will yield different qualities of point on the wiper. A range of wipers, from thick to thin can also prove very useful,

providing the pastel painter with a range of this tool that is not unlike a range of different sizes and quality of brush.

As with all things, practice makes perfect, therefore do not expect to necessarily produce a perfect wiper the first time around. Once you get the hang of rolling these wipers, it does not take long to produce a selection for use at the start of every painting session.

Cut paper to size – approx. 15cm (6″) x 7.5cm (3″). Roll around a pencil.

TIP:

Try different papers for different effects in blending. Try different weights of paper to create tougher or softer blending action. Try different sizes of paper to produce different thicknesses of wiper.

ARTSTRIPS ©

Slip pencil out of one end of the roll. Roll paper between fingers to soften and help it curl more evenly.

Open up roll (do not flatten out). At tightest rolled end (previously innermost), sharply crease in approx. 6mm (¼″) of the edge.

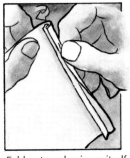

Run fingernail along the centre of the resultant fold to create inward crease.

Fold outer edge in on itself. Previously created creases now form tightly folded centre 'spindle' for rolling the remaining paper around.

Roll paper tightly round the folded centre 'spindle'. Use sticky tape to fix side of wiper. Turn base over and fix with sticky tape to provide a tough end.

NOTE – THE WIPER RARELY ROLLS EVENLY, WHICH IS IDEAL, AS THIS IS HOW THE REQUIRED POINT IS NATURALLY FORMED.

Common problems

STRETCHING PASTEL PAPER

Stretching paper is normally associated with watercolour painting, but is essential if thin pastel paper is to be used with wet underpainting. Pastel paper does not contain as much size as watercolour paper, it will therefore dry faster and be more vulnerable to damage, if mistreated while wet.

Method

Care should be taken when stretching thin pastel paper, which requires gentle handling, especially when rubbing the surface, or pulling it tight when wet.

Being thin, pastel paper does not require much wetting, but it is still better to dip it through water, rather than rub it with a sponge. Although soft, a sponge will damage the paper if applied with too much friction.

Dip the paper into a sink or bath filled with cold water.

IMPORTANT:

Once stretched, the paper should be left on the board until the painting has been fully completed.
To remove the finished pastel, cut away gently, by running a sharp blade through the gumstrip, along the edge of the paper.

Hold paper by one corner and allow excess water to run off until dripping stops. Repeat with opposite corner.

Place paper on an unpainted, unvarnished drawing board. Remove any large air bubbles by gently rubbing with back of hand, or gently pulling paper.

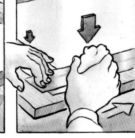

Wet pre-cut lengths of gumstrip by dipping through water. Place over paper – overlapping half of gumstrip along edge of paper, other half along drawing board.

Wipe along its surface with heavily absorbent paper towel to force out and absorb excess water from beneath tape. Use free hand to hold gumstrip in place.

To ensure maximum adhesion, run fingernail down surface of gumstrip, at paper edge. Leave drawing board flat until paper dries.

NOTE – ALWAYS USE GUMSTRIP (GUMMED PARCEL TAPE). NEVER USE MASKING TAPE OR SELF-ADHESIVE PAPER/PLASTIC PARCEL TAPE

Exploiting colour palettes

Colour layering is the most important element in achieving more sophisticated levels of colour mixing within any pastel painting. However, the ability to exploit colour is dependent on the type of pastels being used and their quality, as are the methods of application and particular techniques.

DRY PASTELS, THE SOLE SUBJECT OF THIS BOOK, not to be confused with wax-based or oil pastels, are available in a far wider range of qualities. The better the quality, the more pigment they contain. The more pigment they contain, the purer and more intense the colour.

Most importantly and as a general rule of thumb, the better the quality of pastels, the softer they tend to be. It is this degree of softness that determines to what extent the pastel painter can build up the colours in layers, to effect colour mixing.

Tutorials and exercises in the basics section provided an introduction to the range of colours that could be used to fully exploit the potential of pastels. One exercise showing how a limited palette could be manipulated to considerable effect, through maximising the range of tints in each colour. The other demonstrating how to work with a full colour range, building up from darks to lights.

We now move on in this section to evaluate the efficiency of a set of sketching pastels in achieving colour mixes for a simple exercise. On the other hand, a full range of the softest Artists' Quality pastels takes you into the next stage of development, the ultimate in colour mixing for a full-blown pastel painting.

The issue of softness can be slightly confusing in that the term 'soft' does not in of itself denote the degree of softness. In other words, many pastels are termed soft, whereas some are softer than others. It is left up to the painter to determine which degree of softness is best suited to their particular style and techniques.

The set of sketching pastels employed in the limited colour palette exercise that follows could, therefore, be equally termed 'soft square pastels'. Undoubtedly they are harder than the Artists' Quality soft pastels used in the stage-by-stage painting. Being a boxed set, they come in a limited range of hues (colours).

Being limited in colour, harder and of course somewhat cheaper, I refer to these as sketching pastels. However, as you will experience, they are quite capable of providing some powerful results and this may lead you to feel that they will serve a purpose beyond that of merely sketching pastels. This is a matter of personal choice and perception.

The question is this – can these harder sketching pastels be paired up with the softer Artists' Quality pastels? Indeed they can, but their degree of hardness, will dictate the manner and order in which they can be used. The harder the pastel, the greater the pressure required to apply it. Use a hard pastel over a softer one and the pressure will be just as likely to dislodge the soft colour, as apply the hard colour. The answer is to simply reverse the process, by working soft pastels over hard pastels.

Will the limited hues in the sketching pastels prove to be frustrating?

Having experienced what can be achieved with limited colour ranges, this should not be cause for concern. The following exercise demonstrates that exact colour matching is not necessary to reproduce the effects of light, nor indeed of transparency. Of far more importance is a range of values and with black and white in the set of pastels, these can be easily achieved.

Having experienced how the softness of the pastel and the amount of pigment it contains controls the colour mix, the final element in fully exploiting colour palettes is the surface colour and texture over which the pastel is laid. Whilst in the basics section the surface colour was allowed to invade the final result to some degree, the full colour palette, stage-by-stage painting in this section is concentrated on the texture of the surface.

By customising the surface, the pastel painter can decide on and control the quality and depth of the tooth. What should be remembered is the fact that by creating more texture, the pastel painter is establishing a surface that will take a greater number of layers that can be applied without having to resort to fixing.

The stage-by-stage painting therefore incorporates a surface prepared with acrylic texture/modelling paste that is gently coloured. You will experience first hand how powerfully this sort of surface will accept and display the undercolours, as they are blended in. As the layers are built up into a fluid juicy mix, it allows for scuffing and scumbling, enabling the use of visual colour mixing, rather than physical mixing.

This simply means that the surface colour is broken by the underlying textures, through which the under layers can be seen, even within single pastel strokes.

You will soon discover that the impressionistic colour mixes this creates are always stimulating and surprising, no matter how often the technique is used.

Final layers need not be fixed, so effective is the surface tooth at holding the pastel colours. This allows intense lights and final highlights to sparkle against the duller colours applied earlier.

It is only by comparing the various qualities of pastels that you will discover the differences of pressure need for their application and blending. You will experience how many colour layers are possible with each and at which stage it is appropriate to use black or white.

Exercise

Sketching pastels are usually available in sets of a limited range of colours. Select a smaller range of family colours to work with.

Pick out a light colour. Use pastel tip to draw out symmetrical form in line.

Use flat side edge to block in mid-values as solidly as paper texture allows.

With compressed paper stump, force pastel into surface to create soft directional strokes.

Limited colour range demands use of black for accents.

Black is enriched by overlaying mid-value colours.

Further blending solidifies colour blocks…

…and mixes colour layers. Black re-emerges.

Re-apply mid-value colours to once again add richness to the black.

White rubbed gently into surface gives soft lights (surface mixing).

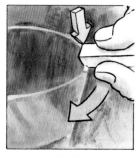

Hard pastel highlights need real pressure to adhere – often causing shape or size of highlights to distort.

To correct, scratch away excess with curved blade of erasing knife.

Limited colour palette

Square sketching pastels are harder than Artists' Quality soft pastels and come in a limited colour range, which demands a bold approach.

Both black and white need to be used more extensively, to bolster the limited number of available pastel pigments. Black provides accents, over which other colours are gently laid, or into which they are mixed. Black is therefore seldom left in its raw state.

White is also similarly worked into other colours, but added to that it is also used in its pure form for final highlights.

Allow the pastel strokes to ride across the texture of the paper, rather than push them fully into its bed. This will encourage you to exploit the surface of the paper as both a colour and as a textural feature. So let it show through the pastel paper wherever it might prove to benefit the end result.

Where solid colour is required, this is achieved through forcing the pastel into the tooth (texture) of the paper. In this exercise, solid colour overwhelms the paper colour to produce the soft dark areas, which provide an excellent foil for the staccato highlight strokes.

Note how the definition along the silhouette edge of the glass varies from hard to soft, dark to light. Although the glass is hard, the surface at its edge recedes. Should the edge become too hard, the glass will appear to stand away from the background. Should the edge become too soft and the glass, rather than being hard in character, will soften to the consistency of cotton-wool.

Stage-by-stage

Full colour palette

A custom-made textured surface was prepared for this painting, the basis of which is a piece of acid-free mount board cut to the required size. The board was firstly primed by vigorously applying a coat of acrylic gesso primer with a bristle brush and then left to dry. Once thoroughly dry, the primed surface was then overlaid with a thin, but continuous, layer of acrylic texture modelling paste, again applied with a bristle brush. As can be seen, the surface is tinted yellow, achieved by gently colouring the acrylic modelling paste, using an acrylic yellow paint.

The resultant surface is ideal for pastel work for a number of reasons. First, the addition of acrylic serves to strengthen the card considerably. Second, the added arbitrary texture, achieved by using random brush-strokes, provides the surface with a substantial tooth, which is vitally important in successfully enabling the build up of a number of layers using Artists' Quality soft pastels. Third, a specific surface colour can be created to maximise the potential of every aspect of the composition, rather than having to work with a pre-determined paper colour.

STAGE 1

Step 1 – Use a dark brown pastel to outline the principal elements within the composition. Since some of the four sides will be lost either under a frame rebate or mount, it is helpful to loosely define the likely extent of this, in order that it can be taken into account when composing the picture. The sketched rectangle therefore shows the inner boundary of the composition.

This is particularly important in this painting, since there is a mountain range at the top which could easily touch the inner edge of the mount or frame, perhaps even disappear altogether, if not correctly positioned.

Step 2 – With a compressed paper stump, vigorously work the brown outline across the surface of the composition. These should be directional strokes carving out the shapes and suggesting the values of the finished piece. Note how much pigment was contained in these simple first strokes. Blending not only suggest volume and value, but also disperses this pigment as a fine layer and presses it into the tooth, making it more stable. Also note that areas such as the middle distance hill (right) and the low foreground bushes have become almost solid, reminding you where the soft darks are to be laid.

NOTE – THIS IS A GOOD POINT AT WHICH TO FIX THE SURFACE USING SPRAY FIXATIVE, IN ORDER THAT THE DRAWING REMAINS INTACT, EVEN WHEN YOU BEGIN THE VIGOROUS BLENDING OF THE MIDDLE LAYERS OF PASTEL.

STAGE 2

The aim of this painting is to maximise a full colour palette using Artists' Quality soft pastels, which requires you to gently move through a full range of values (lights and darks) until the pure white of the highlights is reached. It always difficult at this stage to hold oneself in check, for it is tempting to reach for those lovely bright, light colours offered by the better quality soft pastels. It is essential however to keep to the middle values for as long as possible.

Background and middle distance

At this stage we are lucky enough to have already established some rich darks, which need to be exploited for as long as possible. The purpose now is to overlay them with a thin layer of colour, through which they can be seen. Be restrained when laying gentle strokes of colour, but vigorous in smearing them into and across the surface. Having been fixed, the darks beneath should not be disturbed.

Foreground

This is treated slightly differently. Foliage and bushes will need the darkest accents within the entire composition. Consequently, much heavier deposits of dark warm colours are required. These can still be forced into the surface with a blender. However, blending will need to be carefully controlled and directional, following the lie of the pigment, in order that dark structure and rhythms inherent in the foreground are not lost, by being merged into a solid, shapeless dark mass.

NOTE – WARM AND COOL AREAS ON THE PILLARS AND STONES, AN EARLY INDICATION OF THE WARM AND COOL LIGHTS THAT WILL PLAY ACROSS THEIR WHITE VOLUMES.

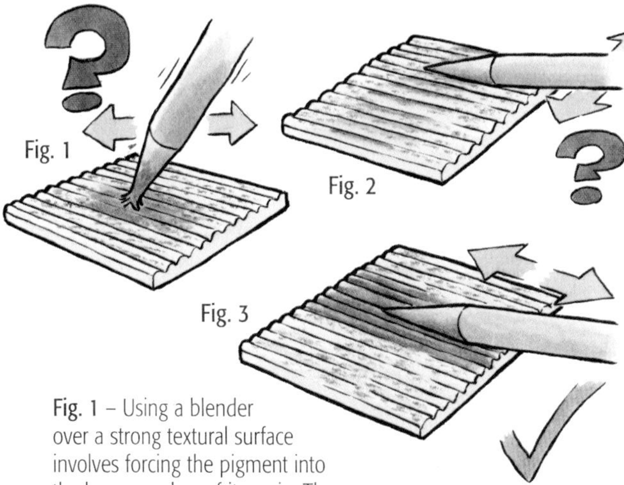

Fig. 1

Fig. 2

Fig. 3

Fig. 1 – Using a blender over a strong textural surface involves forcing the pigment into the lower reaches of its grain. The temptation is to hold the blender at a steep angle, so that its point can deliver the colour. However, the pressure required will swiftly damage the blender point. It is far safer to use the shoulder of the blender.

Fig. 2 – Now you will find that blending across the grain of the brush-stroke will only deposit pigment on their upper reaches.

Fig. 3 – The correct way in which to blend is to use the shoulder of the blender and blend along the grain of the texture. This will enable the blender to penetrate deeper, which is exactly where the dark colours need to be placed.

Edges can be reworked in four different ways to make them appear more natural.

STAGE 3

Move up the values toward those lighter, brighter colours. However, it should be borne in mind that this landscape recedes considerably, creating considerable depth between the foreground foliage and the distant mountain range. Being a Mediterranean scene, it is also drenched in light.

Depth

This requires aerial perspective, where depth is achieved through exploiting colour temperatures. Note the amount of blues used in the mixes, or as undercolour, throughout the colour in the distance. Also note the darkness of the accents when you compare foreground (foliage), middle distance (hills) and background (mountain range). Both colour temperature and accents have to be correctly balanced to attain a good sense of aerial perspective.

Since the background and middle distance need to be painted first, it is always difficult to keep them soft. The urge is to give them contrast and colour. Keep the background gentle and it will not fight with the foreground, which is the focal subject matter. Keep reminding yourself that the background provides a simple backdrop for the bright colours and contrasts of the foreground. If necessary, blend over-excited contrasts or edges, to make them recede.

Note the silhouette edge of the dark hill (middle right). At this stage, a chunk is removed from its centre. As your eye moves along its edge observe how some parts remain sharp, whilst others are blended into softness. This irregularity is much more natural and imparts the feeling that the land has form, rather than being a two-dimensional stage set.

A

A. Blending with a compressed paper stump, rolled paper wiper, brush or finger. Keep blending irregular, allowing an edge to go in and out of focus.

B

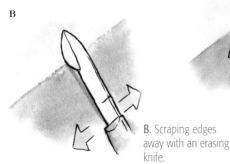

B. Scraping edges away with an erasing knife.

C

C. Blending with a kneadable putty rubber is possible when used lightly. Apply more pressure and it will lift the pastel completely.

D

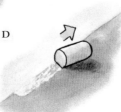

D. Redrawing with a pastel, using a scuff or a more solid stroke to completely move an edge (positive painting). Alternatively, repainting the space around the edge (negative painting) will reshape the subject itself.

STAGE 4

The broken columns need to stand out against the landscape, which means the small rise behind and to the bottom of them needs to be darkened to provide the necessary contrast. A mid-brown should be applied with some pressure and then pushed further into the surface with a compressed paper stump.

The ruins are now given the first layer to take them towards the strong light which hits the various structures from the right hand side. These include a warm pink underlay for the sunlit side. The left hand side however, requires a reflected cool blue light from the sky.

With a mid to dark brown, add accents to sharpen the drawing at selected points around the stonework. This should also extend to the stonework between the foreground foliage and the ruins, which will emphasise its structure, rather than this area appearing as merely a mound of earth. Reinforce this with some black and use to also accent the darks of the bushes and foliage in the foreground.

This completes the accents of the foreground, providing the contrasts required for the flowers to work against. Finally, some pink grasses are introduced behind the bush on the left. Not only does this provide a texture that represents the sunlight coming from the right, but also a complementary contrast for the greens of the foreground foliage.

As the layers of colour deepen, less and less pressure is required to achieve the desired results when blending. The pastel painting surface feels almost fluid, as the soft pigments slide over each other with little friction. To achieve the rounded forms of the columns, graduated colour needs to be laid moving inward from the sharp line of the column edges, dissipating in strength towards their centre line. On the left hand side this is a light blue of reflected light, while on the right it is the pink of warm sunlight.

To achieve this particular effect, first use the sharp edge of a pastel piece to draw in the column edge. This features differing degrees of strength of colour down each edge and requires careful consideration as to where the strongest contrasts are required.

Once these edges have been applied, lay the shoulder of the compressed paper stump over the line of deposited colour and blend inward. Move the blender progressively down the edge, blending the full length of each column.

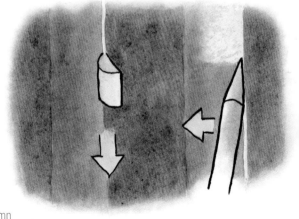

◁   **In the far distance of the background**, the visual excitement created by the tooth of the surface is clearly visible. The dark colours of the sky and mountain have been forced down into the recesses of the texture with a blender. Lighter colours drawn over the surface catch the protruding textures. Viewed from a distance the colours mix visually, however, as you draw closer, note how the surface splinters into Impressionistic patterns. By contrast, the green of the trees to the bottom left are blended, but not overlaid, so appear soft in comparison to the background.

◁   **Here again, arbitrary texture breaks up the pastel strokes** in an unexpected way. The colours beneath are used to effect the solidity of the columns and have been blended smooth. Over this solid base, highlight colours are dispersed unevenly and their vigour stimulates the imagination. The greens behind the columns are not enhanced with a top layer of highlight and consequently they provide a solid background that acts as a counterfoil to the columns. This prevents the silhouettes of the columns from disintegrating into a confusion of highlights.

◁   **The green laid across the foreground** could create a visual wall, which would act like an unnecessary barrier, preventing the viewer from looking further into the painting. The flowers are used to overcome this effect, to provide a welcoming invitation to look further. They do this by leading the eye from the right hand side, moving left to the centre and on into the rest of the painting. This is achieved by showing the flowers at their largest on the right, gradually diminishing in size as they progress left to the centre. The vibrant rhythms in the flowers and foliage also catch the eye, drawing the viewer into the composition.

STAGE 5

This last layer of colour requires little or no blending and is used to suggest focus. The sharp edges of the pastel sticks prove ideal to achieve this.

Middle distance – ruins
These require highlights of blue within the reflected lights and light orange, followed by pure white for the sunlit faces.

Foreground
Foliage leaves are worked up with cool reflected blue-green light in their shadows. Their sunlit areas should be taken toward yellow-greens and eventually into pure yellow.

Flowers
This will have been worth the wait! The flower colours should be kept as pure as possible. Start with mid-value colours and add a highlight to some. The positioning of each flower head needs careful consideration, for not only do the flower masses create rhythms that carry the eye, the shape of each flower head differs in shape, as it does in size. Use a pastel stroke to suggest each flower head, rather than spend time attempting precise detail. This is the very essence of painting, using a single stroke to suggest something much more.

TIP:
Practice a variety of pastel strokes on scraps of paper to produce different shapes and sizes of flower head before committing to the actual painting. Study the shape and movement in a single flower head and attempt to emulate that when applying the stroke.

Common problems

CARE OF PASTEL STICKS

While in the throes of a pastel painting, the painter's concentration is strongly focussed on the painting surface and it is easy to forget what is happening elsewhere. Every artist is prone to building a collection of pastels in the palm of the hand as he or she is working.

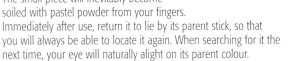

Consequence

Unfortunately, being soft and geared to easily delivering the pigment, pastels held in the palm will soon soil not only the painter's hand, but, more problematically, each other.

Although cleaning one's hands is easy enough, soiled pastels soon prove exceedingly frustrating. Their colour becomes more difficult to identify, especially the difference between tints of the same colour.

In our eagerness to get on with the painting, most of us never lose this tendency entirely. Matters can be alleviated to some degree, by introducing a working practice that will reduce this sort of soiling and confusion in identifying colours and tints.

Solution

It is seldom necessary to utilise a full pastel stick. Better by far to snap off a smaller piece, which is beneficial in allowing you to attain a far wider range of marks by presenting different flat faces and edges of the pastel piece to the surface. The small piece will inevitably become soiled with pastel powder from your fingers. Immediately after use, return it to lie by its parent stick, so that you will always be able to locate it again. When searching for it the next time, your eye will naturally alight on its parent colour.

Setting out pastels in an orderly palette of colours will certainly save you time and cost, not to mention from making mistakes on the surface through picking up an incorrect colour.

Place them in a lined rigid container for safer storage and transportation and just as importantly, a tidier work area when working on a painting.

For a simple and cost-effective solution get a pair of matching plastic trays with a shallow rim – one will form the lid, the other the base. The version depicted, features butcher's trays, although plant trays, seedling trays and the like are equally appropriate, providing they have straight sides.

A piece of corrugated card lines the base. This could also be corrugated plastic, such as that used for shelf liners. The corrugated liner needs to be cut to size and should not buckle.

The pastel sticks will now lie snugly in the corrugations, separated from each other and therefore keeping clean.

For added safe storage and transportation, lining the lid with bubble-wrap or a layer of sponge will provide a secure cushion to keep the sticks in place. Secure the lid with an elastic band or another form of fastening.

NOTE – THIS PALETTE OF COLOURS HAS BEEN LAID OUT TO MIMIC THE ORDER IN WHICH THEY APPEAR ON THE COLOUR CIRCLE.

Common problems

MAXIMISING BLACK, WHITE AND COLOUR TEMPERATURE

Should black and white be used in pastel mixing and if so, what is the best method for applying them? These questions are universal, for all painters have experienced the fact that both of these colours can have a dulling effect on mixtures of colour.

Answer

In pastel paintings, however, these two colours are incredibly useful, especially when the range of colours available to the painter is limited. However, just as in working with paints, if either black or white are intermixed too freely with the colour pigments they will dull them down. When it comes to underpainting, this may not pose a problem, since a dull bottom layer is often required in a pastel painting.

Maximising black and white

But what happens when a colour requires darkening or lightening, while needing to retain its intensity? For example, in a flower head where both the highlights and shadows would remain bright?

In these two examples one purple pigment is used [A]. White is used as the underpainting on one swatch of pastel paper [B] while another is underpainted with black [C]. The purple [A] is now applied to completely cover the underpainting on each of the swatches. Although the under-laid colours do not mix with the overlaid purple, each neutral colour does affect the original value of the purple's original hue. The white underpainting makes it lighter [D], while the black underpainting makes it darker [E]. Neither underpainting, however, affects the intensity of the purple.

Maximising colour temperature

Exploiting colour temperature will provide an exciting addition to your repertoire of techniques, when building pastel layers from dark to light. Although simply using successive tints of the same colour will prove adequate, there are instances when the area being painted requires a little more vim and vigour.

It is more visually exciting to be able to identify every layer, as each does its job in creating volume or depth. This is achieved by employing successive layers of warm and cool colours, known as colour temperature change.

Try out this simple exercise for yourself to experience the effects of manipulating colour temperatures.

1 - Use a warm dark brown to draw the initial silhouette.
2 - Follow this with a cool dark green that is slightly lighter in value than the brown. The use of a cool colour over a warm one makes it immediately apparent how one colour is working against the other.
3 - For the third layer, switch to a warm colour, using a lighter value of the colour than that selected for the second layer. You are therefore not only maximising the colour temperatures, but also working through increasingly lighter values.
4 - Finally, apply the cool accents

TIP:

Scumble the pastel strokes, rather than apply them too heavily, so that you can see down through all the layers, even at the lightest points.

NOTE – SOME BLENDING WILL BE REQUIRED AT THE OUTER EDGES OF EACH SUCCESSIVE NEW COLOUR TO HELP CREATE THE ROUNDED FORM OF THE APPLE.

Discovering surface texture

Pastel pigment is totally dependent on the surface for its stability. The surface will provide structure to what is otherwise merely coloured powder. As such, it must be one of the first considerations when determining how any particular subject is to be tackled.

FINDING THE RIGHT SURFACE IS JUST AS IMPORTANT as determining which pastels are best suited to your needs and techniques. Luckily there are many types on offer, from pastel papers to boards, available in predetermined colours and texture,

Although colours vary from black to white, with all possible tints and hues in between, it is usually the mid-values that are most useful. For with these it is possible to not only work from mid lights to darks, but also from mid lights to light. Colours can be balanced much more easily against a mid-tone, as opposed to colours closer to white or black.

Textures vary tremendously, but the most versatile tend to be those that are more amorphous. Heavy or regular textures have their place, but are inclined to become more dominant than the image. The rule of thumb is this, if the texture adds quality or character to a subject, then it is appropriate; if it overpowers the subject, then quite simply the end result will not be right.

Tutorials and exercises in the basics section covered the possibilities of altering surfaces to better suit individual requirements. Showing how the colour of the surface could be changed several times within one painting, through the use of watercolour paint. Although the colour was changed, the texture of the original paper remained. Another approach was to utilise acrylic texture/modelling paste to alter the texture of the surface alone, with colour being provided from another source, the pastels.

This is now taken a step further, by controlling both the colour and texture of the surface.

Acrylic paint is one of the strongest mediums available and forms the basis of the exercise. The acrylic polymer, the glue which carries the pigments, dries by evaporation. In essence, the pigment within a tube of acrylic paint is encased in fluid plastic, which renders it both strong and flexible when dry.

As such, acrylic paint can be applied to almost any surface, from paper to metal, which makes it ideal as a method of preparing an array of surfaces for use in pastel painting. This extends the possibilities considerably and places many dynamic options at the pastel painter's disposal. Acrylic texture/modelling paste is used to provide deeper impasto qualities in the exercise which follows.

What are the benefits in using acrylics to establish a base surface layer?

First of all, strength, since any surface that is strong will hold the pastel colour well, particularly where textures are sharp edged.

Second, the ability to produce dark, dull colours – easily achieved with acrylic paints. These dark, dull mixes provide a far stronger contrast than even the darkest values of pastel pigments, which tend to remain intense.

Third and probably most importantly, acrylic paints offer pastel painters the opportunity to develop unique, painterly textures. Since the paint is applied with a brush, the brush-strokes themselves form a patina across the surface. This is especially true of stiff bristle brushes, which imbue each stroke with a striated surface structure.

Since acrylic paint dries by evaporation, it is inevitable that some depth within these strokes is lost, as the paint shrinks. This should be borne in mind when working with them and steps taken to ensure the brush is well loaded to compensate for this shrinkage.

Once present across the surface, these acrylic brush-strokes provide the tooth required to hold the pastel firm. The deeper and more vigorous the brushwork, the more pastel it can carry.

Not only does this establish a firm base, but the strokes also remain visible and when pastel colours are subsequently stroked across their surface, they become enhanced. The pastel colour scuffs the uppermost surface of the strokes, leaving the acrylic paint to provide darker contrasts in the grooves.

The surface is immediately imbued with the brushy quality of fluid paintwork. Many viewers would be hard-pressed to differentiate between a pastel produced in this way and an oil painting.

Thus, through combining the rich lustre of pure pastel pigments with the unique characteristics of acrylic paints, one of the most dynamic properties of oil painting is mimicked to great effect - the ability to exploit layers of colour.

The stage-by-stage painting goes on to explore the ultimate technique in controlling the surface – decollage for pastel.

While collage is the technique of building up various materials on the surface, decollage is the reverse, it is more akin to sculpting into a surface. Layers of pastel paper are bonded together and then systematically carved through to form a three-dimensional surface onto which the pastel is laid.

The use of pastel paper ensures a good surface colour, which is further enhanced and strengthened by the application of dark acrylic washes.

Once again, the perfect balance of colour, strength and texture has been established to provide an ideal base on which the pastel can be worked.

Exercise

ACRYLIC UNDERPAINTING
Draw out composition on stretched sheet of pastel paper. Boldly block in masses using limited range of acrylic colours.

Build up textured acrylic paint in layers. Concentrate on changes of value. The textured surface should feature flat darks and raised highlights.

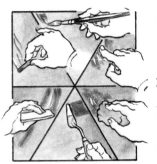

A variety of textures can be achieved by applying the paint with different tools. i.e. brush, finger, sponge, knife, cardboard, stick.

Blend wet acrylic colours with a brush or… reverse brush and use end of shaft to scratch colours together [sgraffito blend]. Allow acrylic painting to dry thoroughly.

PASTEL OVERPAINTING – With Artists' Quality soft pastels, block in dark values (top) and vigorously push or blend them into the surface (bottom).

Fix this layer so that dark pigments bind together, like paint. The applied pastel will become a little transparent through fixing.

As middle and light values are applied, fixing will continue to allow undercolours to show through – use to dull or darken as required.

A kneadable putty rubber can be used to gently rediscover the underpainting beneath unfixed layers. Try such partial erasure of the top layers.

Surface can be gently rubbed with a piece of sandpaper, or pumice…

…to reveal sections of the lighter acrylic highlights surrounded by the softer colours of the pastel.

Light pastel colours can be altered by the nature of the colour beneath. E.g. yellow over blue = cool yellow : yellow over orange = warm yellow.

Should colours become too bright too soon, gently overpaint with greys to dull them down. This will now provide a neutral contrast to other colours.

Textured acrylic underpainting

At first glance this pastel study might appear to be an oil painting. The colours throughout can be seen to be composed of brush-like strokes. However, this is an illusion, as the strokes are the result of an acrylic underpainting layer, applied to create a structured tooth for the pastel layers.

Not only is the acrylic used to provide texture, but it is also used to produce a dark dull undercolour, over which the rich pastel colours can glow.

You need to add acrylic texture/ modelling paste to the acrylic colour mix; otherwise it will not be possible to attain the depth of impasto required, were acrylic paint to be used on its own. The varied depth of texture catches the eye and makes the final painting more dynamic – compare the depth of the tree trunks to that of the sky.

Dark colours are always better flat, but highlights become excited when scattered with as much impasto texture as can be mustered.

This is very much the approach employed in oil painting and at this stage the two media are very much alike. Pastel painting can provide the catalyst to painting in oils, which is but a short step away.

Stage-by-stage

STAGE 1 – BUILDING PAPER LAYERS

1 - Stretch a sheet of white watercolour paper on a strong wooden board. Gather six sheets of pastel paper and enough acrylic medium, or PVA adhesive, to bond these together.

2 - Dip the first sheet of pastel paper into water and having allowed excess water to run off, set to one side on a waterproof surface.

4 - Gently lay the wetted pastel paper on top of the watercolour paper, ensuring you present the adhesive coated surface of the pastel paper to the water-colour paper surface. Lightly ease out any bubbles that may have become trapped under the pastel paper.

Carved surface : decollage

Collage is the technique of building up layers of different material on a base surface. Decollage is the very opposite and involves going down through various layers of applied material. The former provides an image in relief, the latter an image that is carved out [intaglio]. This painting uses the process of carving through strata of bonded paper layers, to create a surface onto which subsequent painted layers can be applied, in this case layers of pastels.

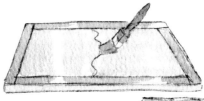

3 - Brush a coat of acrylic medium (or PVA adhesive) across the surface of the stretched watercolour paper and across the upper surface of the wetted pastel paper.

TIP:
Should the glue absorb too swiftly into a pastel sheet already affixed to the board, you can first wet the pastel paper by using either a water-loaded brush, or a misting sprayer.

5 - Take care not exert too much pressure, as the adhesive might squeeze out from between the two wet sheets. Leave to dry thoroughly – the board must be left flat. Repeat the gluing, layering and bonding process with each successive sheet.

ESTABLISHING COMPOSITION

Step 1 – Use a pencil to loosely sketch out the composition.

Do not worry about making changes, since most of the surface will be eventually cut away as the decollage proceeds. Think of this as a scribble, rather than a drawing and you will probably enjoy it more. To correct mistakes, either erase any unwanted marks, or simply strengthen those that are required.

Step 2 – The drawing is now tightened up in ink, although there is still no need to worry about imperfections. After all, the real drawing is to be carried out with a knife. Use a Rigger brush, brush pen or a felt tip for this drawing, whichever you find most comfortable. Preferably the ink should be waterproof, although this is not essential if none is to hand. Since the surface will be rewetted, a non-waterproof ink may run. The pastels will of course cover any runs, but you may find them distracting as you work.

STAGE 2 – DECOLLAGE

The ink drawing serves as your guide for cutting down through the layers of paper. It is important to remember that there are six layers of coloured pastel paper, with the watercolour paper beneath and it is only these pastel paper sheets that you will be cutting through. On no account must the watercolour paper base layer be breached. The bonded sheets of paper should now be exceedingly strong and it is unlikely that they would disintegrate.

Although the depth of the decollage carving needs to be well controlled, to prevent any damage; the possibilities for creating myriad effects are limitless. Experiment with different tools and techniques.

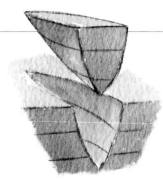

Diagonal cuts meet below the surface, enabling a slice to be cleanly removed. Varying the angles of the cuts will yield different thicknesses of slice. This cutting is tough on any blade and great care should be taken to ensure it does not snap.

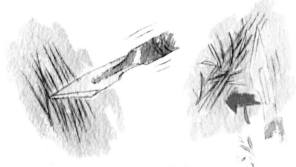

Several cuts, made either directly down into the surface, or at a slight angle, intersect in a shredding motion. Slivers of paper begin to lift from the surface and are shaved away, using the flat of the blade.

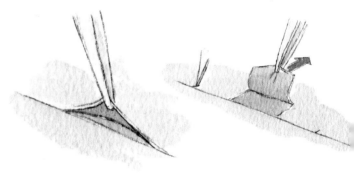

Sharp edges of an object are cut and peeled away with tweezers. However it is easy to lose control of the tear as it can travel in several directions at once. It is therefore better to remove small sections at a time, by making small cuts along the length of the cut line.

To remove a larger section, first cut carefully around the whole area. Small tears may now be made within this section, without them travelling in unwanted directions.

Another method for stopping a tear in its tracks is to simply apply finger pressure in its path. The resultant torn edge, as it reaches the finger, will be more irregular than one that is cut.

Tweezers can be used to nibble at the surface, to lift a lump of paper or tear it away completely.

STAGE 2

Imagine as you cut into the surface that you
are carving down into soft deep shadow,
forming gullies and channels into which an
underpainting of acrylic paint will flow as it
is being applied. Having been disturbed by
the carving process, the exposed surfaces in
these areas will also now become the most
absorbent. Taking on the characteristics of
blotting paper, they will absorb the dark
colours of the acrylic paint and soft pastel
underpainting. In the process, this will
provide the rich accents that are essential
contrasts for the bright pastels to follow.

Use the carving to not only model
objects within the composition, but also
to enliven their characteristics and create
textural relief. The initial cutting may at
first lift and expose only one or two layers
of paper, resulting in a surface that might
require further work. Be experimental in
using various forms of carving, such as
cutting, scraping, nipping and scratching to
fine-tune the desired texture and modelling.

Curtains and window frames
The sections are sliced more evenly to
represent the smooth folds of material or
light reflected from the smooth surface
of the painted frames. Once the slices
are removed therefore, there is no need
to rework the inner levels of the cuts. However, the
triangular gap below the slightly parted curtains reveals
a room beyond and this is reworked to suggest a
shadowy space.

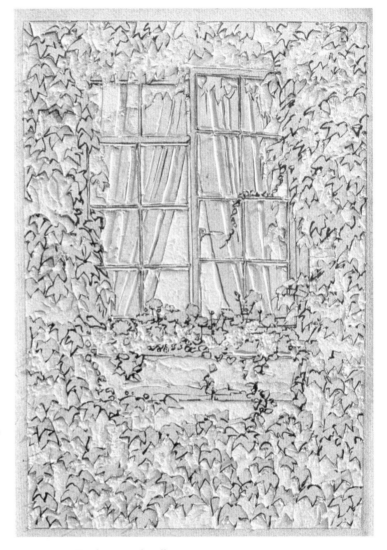

Ivy leaves and wall
Those leaves left uncut stand proud of the wall and
the cut spaces between them must suggest both leaves
behind them and the brick and stonework of the wall
itself. These textures are soft, since they will be deep in
the shadow of the top leaves.

Flowers
The surface of the flower heads are left uncut, so that
the pastel will have a smooth surface against which to
glow, when their colourful accents are applied.

STAGE 3 – UNDERPAINTING

The carving will have loosened and softened the paper layers, the surface therefore needs to be stabilized before work commences with the soft pastels. Although dry dark pastel colour could be worked over the surface, the paper fibres have been exposed and are more inclined to absorb a fluid medium.

Fluid washes of dark acrylic paint fit the bill exactly, for they will also act as a glue to adhere any loose paper that could have been dislodged or is hanging from the surface (Fig A). These fluid washes will also sink into the open paper fibres. Since the torn areas are meant to represent shadow, this is precisely where the soft dark colours are required. Once the acrylic paint has dried, these soft areas will also harden, their surface once again stiff and able to grip the soft pastels more efficiently.

The colour mixes are generally cool, the greens having crimson reds in their mixes to turn them towards grey. Make the mixes fluid, in order that they flood the surface, seeking out loose particles and sinking into the paper fibres.

Fig A

STAGE 4 – SOFT PASTELS

Darks Commence with the darkest of greens and push them down into the lower dark valleys of the surface texture. Within the window, a dark grey-blue is used to suggest greater depth in the interior of the room. A dark red to the flower heads and a dark brown to the window box/plant trough complete the soft darks.

Mid-values and highlights Most of the middle lights and highlights are now built on the higher levels of the surface texture. Note the irregular application of the yellow-greens, which form a loose oval to frame the window.

The white of the window and the red of the flower heads are applied with the maximum pressure, to achieve the most intense colour. These are designed to pull the eye towards them as focal points in the composition.

Common problems

Solution

In the process of working on a pastel painting, it is essential that your hand is prevented from smearing the delicate surface. The solution is to work with the drawing board in an upright position, which is beneficial on two counts. Firstly, you are less likely to catch the painting with your hand, or indeed with your clothing, an all too often inadvertent cause of damage. Secondly, excess pastel crumbs, which occur as pastel strokes are being applied, will fall straight down out of harms way and not onto the surface, as they would do were you working on the flat.

However, if working in an upright position is not suitable and working on the flat is what you prefer, a few simple precautionary measures will make all the difference to your enjoyment of working with pastels.

Should neither of these options be to hand, revert to the basic method of placing a piece of paper directly onto the surface, as a surface on which to rest your hand. It is advisable to utilise the smoothest paper available for this to avoid any chance of creating friction. When the paper needs to be moved to another area, it is essential not to slide the piece across. Instead –

1 Lift the piece directly off the surface.
2 Check the underside for any pastel pigment that may have been lifted off with the paper.
3 Should it be dirty, replace with a clean sheet. You cannot afford to transfer colour from one area to another.
4 Gently and directly lower the support paper onto the next area to be worked on.

CAUTION

Sideways movement on even the smallest area of a pastel painting should be avoided to prevent damage.

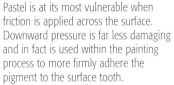

Pastel is at its most vulnerable when friction is applied across the surface. Downward pressure is far less damaging and in fact is used within the painting process to more firmly adhere the pigment to the surface tooth.

One simple option is to use a sturdy ruler placed over two objects of a similar depth/height – e.g. two rolls of tape. When working in an upright position an oil painter's maulstick is the answer.

TIP:
To make your own maulstick, compress a quantity of sponge to form a ball shaped cushion and bind this to one end of a length of bamboo or dowelling.

Common problems

TAKING CARE OF PASTEL PAINTINGS

Ideally a finished pastel sketch or painting should be immediately framed under glass. If this is not possible the question of storage needs careful consideration, otherwise the vulnerable work is liable to damage.

Framing

This is by far the safest method. However, there is nothing more frustrating than going through the process, only to find that particles of pastel powder have become dislodged and are now either clinging to the inside of the glass, lying along the bottom edge of the mount aperture, or along the inner edge of the frame.

Before placing the work into a frame take the following precautionary measure. Gently tap the back of the pastel to dislodge any pastel powder or stray fragments that are clinging loosely to the surface.

Storing

It is not always practical however to have a frame ready and waiting, in which case the pastel sketch or painting will need to be stored safely away. Indeed there may be instances where sketches are produced as a preparatory piece for a future, more complete painting and as such will not be framed.

Again, it must be remembered that sideways friction will damage the work, whilst downward pressure should not. Following this principle, some forms of pastel sketchbooks, or sketchpads, are produced with pages of interleaving smooth paper. Sketches produced in these are less likely to suffer damage, since their surfaces are protected by these sheets.

The same approach is adopted for storing larger pieces on a shelf, in a drawer or in a portfolio – interleaving sheets of smooth paper, such as a shiny lightweight card. The interleaving sheets should be slightly larger than the sketches or paintings over which they are laid.

Several pieces can be stored on top of each other, since the downward weight should not prove damaging to the work itself. However, care must be taken when handling pastel work stored in this way. Remembering that it is sideways movement which causes friction, thus disturbing the surface pastel, gently remove each sheet, by directly lifting it upwards in one motion.

Another option is to custom design a storage system that suits your particular needs and circumstances. One possibility, which not only proves invaluable for storage, but also for transporting work, is based on the same principle as that used with oil paintings – a pair of canvas carriers.

1. Cut two pieces of thin plywood to the same size.
2. Cut two lengths of battens. These should be the same length as the longest edge of the plywood sheets.
3. Pin or glue one batten to the longest edge of one plywood sheet, the other to the longest edge of the second sheet. The battens are there to create a gap between the two sheets of plywood when placed face to face. Pastel sketches or paintings should be pinned to the same face of the plywood sheet, as that to which the batten is fixed.
4. Place the top of both plywood sheets within the carrying handle section of the canvas carriers.
5. Place the bottom of both plywood sheets within the foot section of the canvas carriers.

Not only does this system provide a method of carrying pastels, the handle itself can be used to hang this storage pack out of harms way.

TIP:
Should you wish to have a pastel painting framed professionally it is important to bear in mind that the framer will want to take steps to protect the work from possible damage whilst in their care.

Some are likely to apply fixative to the surface of the work, which will be to the detriment of the final layers that you have so painstakingly produced. In essence this action would dull and flatten the final lights and highlights and should be avoided!

Take the painting to the framers, make your choice and agree on the completion date. Inform the framers that you will take the painting home and will bring it back to have it mounted in position and placed in the frame.

Useful information

PAINTING KIT NEEDED TO COMPLETE THE TUTORIALS IN THIS BOOK

Paul Taggart's exercises and tutorials in this book take readers through a variety of techniques, from working with a basic boxed set of sketching pastels through to producing paintings using Artists' Quality soft pastels. The materials required to complete these exercises have therefore been broken down into manageable kits, which should enable painters to work at their own pace and progressively add materials as required.

BASIC START-UP KIT
[Limited Colour Palette]

Pastels (pages 16–17)
  Square Sketching Pastels [Limited Palette] – Boxed Set

Artists' Quality soft pastels [Limited Palette]
  Brown – with warm bias [at least 6 tints from lightest towards dark]
  Blue – with warm bias [at least 6 tints from lightest towards dark]
  Black
  White

Blenders (pages 24–25, 58–59)
  Round Watercolour Brush
  Compressed Paper Stumps
  Rubber Tipped Pastel Blenders

Pastel Paper (pages 40–41)
Spray Fixative (page 57)
Pastel Erasing Knife (pages 72–76)
Kneadable Putty Rubber (page 56)
Drawing Board
Gumstrip 50mm (2") (page 69)

BASIC START-UP KIT
[Full Colour Palette]

Pastels (additional to those in the Limited Colour Palette) – range of tints from lightest to dark *Artists' Quality soft pastels* [Primary and Secondary Colours Palette]

PRIMARIES
Red-purple (warm red)
Red-orange (cool red)
Blue-purple (warm blue)
Blue-green (cool blue)
Yellow-orange (warm yellow)
Yellow-green (cool yellow)

SECONDARIES
Green
Orange
Purple

Watercolour Paper
Waterproof Indian Ink [Black]
Rigger Brush
Bristle Brush
Acrylic Texture/Modelling Paste
Oil Painting Knife

OPTIONAL UNDERPAINTING MATERIALS
Watercolour Paints
Acrylic Paints
Lightfast, Waterproof Felt Tip Pen
Waterproof Lightfast Brush Pen

OCCASIONAL GLOSSARY

TECHNIQUES
Impasto
Applied paint/paste layers that creates physical texture on the painting surface.

Sgraffito
Scratching into a soft layer of pastel or wet paint with a pointed tool.

Hatching
Parallel strokes of line applied in clusters to create textured shading.

Cross-Hatching
Overlaid or interwoven hatching used to create progressively darker shaded areas.

Wet on Dry
Paint applied to a dry surface resulting in brushmarks that dry with a hard, clean edge, even when applied lightly.

Scuff
Dragged stroke of colour deposited irregularly.

Scumble
A number of scuffs merging together to cover a wider area.

COLOUR REFERENCES (Pastels)
A diagrammatic representation of the relative positions of the intense primary and secondary colours.

Hue
Hue is a bright primary or secondary colour on the basic colour circle.

Complementary Colours
Colours that lie exactly opposite to one another across the colour circle.

Value
Value is the degree of lightness or darkness of a colour.

Tone
Tone is the degree of lightness or darkness of a neutral grey.

Lights
The lightest hue of colour in any particular section of a painted area.

Highlights
The tiny point of light on the surface at which the light source is reflected. This reflected light maybe white, or a colour.

Accents
The darkest points of shadow of an object.

Tints
Colour plus white.

Shades
Colour plus black.

Local Colour
The colour of an object under normal daylight conditions.

Colour Temperature
The suggestion of warmth or coolness conveyed to varying degrees by all colours.

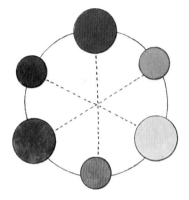

TERMS

Intaglio
A furrowed surface into which pigment can be laid.

Aerial Perspective
A sense of distance, usually within a landscape, caused by diminishing colour values and colour temperature.

Negative Painting
Painting the space around an object, rather than the object itself.

Arbitrary Texture
Impasto laid with multi-directional strokes unrelated to the structure or form of the subject.

Structural Texture
Impasto laid with directional strokes to suggest the structure and form of the subject.

Reflected Light
The cool highlight seen within shadowed areas.

ART WORKSHOP WITH PAUL
Tuition and Guidance for the Artist in Everyone

Log on to the artworkshopwithpaul.com website for downloadable tutorials and Art Clinic, relating to working with watercolours, oils, acrylics, pastels, drawing and other media.

Check out Paul's Bookshelf for details of all his books. Visit *Paul's Gallery* and the various galleries showing original paintings, limited edition prints, commissioned work, examples of collected works and work in progress.

Catch up on the latest news and details of Art Workshop With Paul Taggart Painting Breaks & Courses.

Alternatively you can write to
Art Workshop With Paul Taggart / FS
c/o Promark, Studio 282, 24 Station Square, Inverness, Scotland, IV1 1LD

Or email
mail@artworkshopwithpaul.com

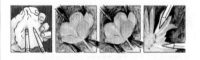

Artstrips©
Fully narrated and detailed step-by-step demonstrations form the basis of all Paul Taggart's live tutorials.

To translate these into publishable form was his ambition and thus it was that twenty years ago he conceived of the Artstrips©.

Unique to Paul Taggart, these Artstrips© are intended as a universally understood method of visually conveying detailed instructions.

Paul Taggart

Fine Artist & Author Paul Taggart

From his home in the Northern Highlands of Scotland, professional Fine Artist & Author Paul Taggart shares his enthusiasm for painting with a global audience, through the many books he has written and his extensive website. Paul Taggart's passion for art started at a very early age and ever since gaining a degree in Fine Art over thirty years ago has enjoyed the patronage of collectors, who have purchased an extensive collection of original paintings and limited edition prints.

In line with his belief that everyone should be encouraged to express themselves creatively, Paul Taggart considers it a privilege to have been able to work with aspiring artists throughout that period and to continue to do so. His aim is to provide the right sort of practical help and encouragement in a 'no-nonsense' style that makes the pursuit of painting and drawing accessible to all.

His extensive knowledge across all media in these fields proves invaluable to those following his tutorials, whether through books, the website or when attending his painting breaks and workshops.

Watercolours, oils, acrylics, pastels, drawing and mixed media – all can be developed through Paul Taggart's thorough method of tutoring, honed over many decades of listening to aspiring artists and understanding what they need to achieve their pursuit.

Art Workshop With Paul Taggart is the banner under which Paul Taggart offers a variety of learning aids, projects and events, which include books, videos, internet tutorials, painting breaks and courses.

ACKNOWLEDGEMENTS

Key people have played a major role in my life and in whom I place my unreserved trust - to them, as always, I say a heartfelt thank you. Eileen (my Life & Business Partner) and I, are delighted to dedicate this series of books to someone who has brought them to life, who wholeheartedly joined us in our work some while ago and now gets to see the fruits of her labours – Sunita Gahir. Since setting the design style for my previous series of six books, she has become an invaluable friend, both privately and professionally.

My professional life is split into painting a body of collectable originals, fulfilling commissions, producing material for books and my website, as well as tutoring aspiring painters in painting breaks etc. It is only through the continued patronage of collectors and demand for tutoring from painters that my life as a Professional Fine Artist can continue. Not forgetting those publishers with whom I share a mutual professional trust – most particularly Robert and Susan Guy of Sandcastle Books, who got this series off to a flying start.

Paul Taggart